Crisis & Trauma

In Colleges and Universities

Edited by
Russell Lee and Dan Casey

CHEVRON
PUBLISHING CORPORATION

Printed in the United States of America

ISBN: 1-883581-41-9

CHEVRON
PUBLISHING CORPORATION
5018 Dorsey Hall Drive, Suite 104
Ellicott City, MD 21042
410-740-0065

Crisis & Trauma

In Colleges and Universities

Edited by
Russell Lee and Dan Casey

CHEVRON
PUBLISHING CORPORATION

About the Authors

Stephen R. Bennett, Psy.D., L.P., is Director of the Counseling Center, Gustafus Adolphus College, St. Peter, Minnesota.

Dan Casey, Ed.D., is Director of Crisis Management Counseling and Consultation, a firm specializing in trauma and crisis response in Clear Lake, Minnesota.

Beth Doshan is a Behavior Analyst III and Community Behavior Crisis Consultant at the Minnesota Neurorehabilitation Hospital for the State of Minnesota, Department of Human Services.

Raymond B. Flannery, Jr., Ph.D., is Associate Clinical Professor of Psychology, Department of Psychiatry, Harvard Medical School, and a staff member of the Massachusetts Department of Mental Health, Boston, Massachusetts.

Kendall Johnson, Ph.D., is a school consultant, family therapist, and teacher in a high school for at-risk students. He lives in Claremont, California.

Russell Lee, Ed.D., is Professor and Chair of the Psychology Department and Director of the Center for Professional Development at Bemidji State University in Bemidji, Minnesota.

Judith Putzel Price, Ed.D., is Associate Director of the Counseling Center at Keene State College in Keene, New Hampshire.

Contents

Introduction ix

CHAPTER 1
Case Study of the Tornado at Gustavus Adolphus College 1
Stephen R. Bennett, Psy.D., L.P.

CHAPTER 2
Traumatic Stress Disorders 13
Russell Lee, Ed.D.

CHAPTER 3
Vicarious Traumatization 29
Beth Doshan

CHAPTER 4
The Effects of Trauma on Post-Secondary Learning 45
Kendall Johnson, Ph.D.

CHAPTER 5
Working with Parents of College and University Students 59
Russell Lee, Ed.D.

CHAPTER 6
Critical Incident Stress Management: The Core Components 71
Dan Casey, Ed.D.

CHAPTER 7
Pre-Crisis Plans: The Development of a
Crisis Response Team 89
Dan Casey, Ed.D.

CHAPTER 8
During the Crisis 105
Dan Casey, Ed.D.

CHAPTER 9
Crisis Intervention in the College and
University Community: The Assaulted Staff
Action Program (ASAP) 113
Raymond B. Flannery, Jr., Ph.D.

CHAPTER 10
Summary Chapter – Epilogue 127
Dan Casey, Ed.D., and Judith Putzel Price, Ed.D.

APPENDIX
Role Play Scenarios 131
Dan Casey, Ed.D.

Index 141

Introduction

One of the editors was, some time ago, the director of a bustling university counseling center that consisted of fifteen professional staff, and that offered a wide range of therapeutic and developmental services. Staff morale was high, and there was a strong sense of shared purpose and mission. We felt that we were serving students well. Within a couple of years of his leaving that position the budget crunch that higher education is still facing hit, and that institution, although its enrollment has grown, now has reduced its counseling center staff to two therapists.

In addition, the student body has changed. Improvements in psychotropic medication have resulted in students now on campus whose disorders would have made them unable to attend in prior years. Those two therapists tend to be booked most of the day, seeing the students with the most serious and long-term diagnoses. Waiting times for new appointments are lengthy. Students experiencing transitory stresses, even acute stress disorder, may not be seen for over a month. This is now a usual story for most college counseling centers.

Student life has changed as well. Campus stresses and campus tragedies have increased. In this post 9/11 era we are aware of the human cost of terrorism, and that cost is added to the cost of school shootings, school violence, and even natural disasters. Given the pressures of grades and exams, students are vulnerable to the added stress of campus disasters. College and university personnel, whether teaching, in administration, or providing student support services, need to be aware of rapid, effective techniques that can help students cope with crises.

This book has been written because we feel there is not a publication available today that addresses the unique needs of higher education facilities in times of crisis.

We do not offer a detour around suffering. Instead, we offer a path to take and directions to follow to guide any higher education institution in the management of traumatic events that occur on campus or that occur elsewhere but affect campus personnel.

The book does not offer therapy, nor does it take the place of therapy.

It describes, in detail, crisis intervention techniques that can be used prior to, during and following traumatic events. This crisis intervention textbook will guide administrators and counselors, as well as campus security, residential staff, and faculty through a crisis event.

The interventions suggested in this book are based on the International Critical Incident Stress Foundation's expertise and research over the last 20 years. Each of the interventions described have been used extensively and have proven to be the best model available for crisis intervention in general, and in colleges and universities in particular.

Each chapter in the book is developed specifically toward crisis intervention and crisis management from the college and university perspective. Case histories are shared that show some of the crisis events that have occurred where crisis intervention techniques have been used very successfully. How crisis effects the way students think and react, how staff and faculty are affected by the event, as well as exactly what type of intervention fits in the event timetable and typical expected reactions are addressed in specific chapters. Vicarious traumatization is identified and addressed.

What we have written and shared is a blend of our experiences and the research completed at the time of this printing. Our personal insights come from resolving a number of crisis reactions following traumatic events over the years. Although we begin with a case study of Gustavus Adolphus College, for the most part the names and identifying details have been changed to protect confidentiality.

CHAPTER 1

Case Study of the Tornado at Gustavus Adolphus College

By Stephen R. Bennett, Psy.D., L.P.

"This is just stuff. We're lucky to be alive."
(March 29, 1998 tornado survivor)

"There isn't a house in the area" near Gustavus Adolphus College *"that didn't suffer damage, was pulled off its foundation or was completely destroyed. It was total devastation, a very sobering sight."*
(An eyewitness account of the March 29, 1998 tornado)

"There are victories of the soul and spirit. Because of these, sometimes even when you lose, you win."
(A quote by Elie Wisel posted on a wall outside of the campus Telecommunications Office at Gustavus Adolphus College—Spring, 1998)

On Sunday, March 29, 1998, at 5:27 p.m. the warning sirens sounded to alert the 10,000 residents of St. Peter, a rural farming community in Southern Minnesota, and home to Gustavus Adophus College, to take shelter from a fast moving tornado that was gathering momentum as it moved with destructive force across the prairie. A local police officer on patrol that afternoon on the outer edge of town spotted a massive funnel cloud on the eastern horizon gobbling up crops, barns, and pieces of the spring landscape as it moved with powerful force westward toward the town of St. Peter. He called the dispatcher to sound the outdoor siren, hoping that advanced warning would give area residents a little more time to take cover from the massive wall cloud that was rapidly approaching (Rosario, 1999).

Then the tornado hit. A 1¼-mile wide tornado, an F3 on the Fujita-Pearson tornado intensity scale, packing winds of up to 200 miles per hour cut a swath through the heart of campus and town on its westward path of destruction. Eyewitnesses at the epicenter of the storm tell chilling stories of what it was like to be in the middle of this devastation. Familiar themes about the sky turning black as if it were suddenly midnight at 5:30 PM, and the wind howling like a freight-train barreling down the tracks. Windows were blown in, 100-year-old trees uprooted, and buildings leveled in an instant.

College Crises

The unfortunate and inevitable reality for college and university officials is that campus crises occur. The nature of the crisis will vary depending upon a number of issues, for instance, the setting, i.e., rural as opposed to metro sites, the size of the college or university, and the clientele who attend the college or university. The college that has most of the students living in dormitories on campus will experience a different set of crises events compared to a college that has mostly older than average students who drive from home to school each day. This also is affected by the age of the students. Younger students in states that have a legal drinking age of 21 years have and are involved in crises that differ significantly from colleges where the mean age of students is older than the legal drinking age. Issues such as accidental death, suicide, attempted suicide, homicide, binge drinking, sexual assaults, physical violence, illnesses, fire, and natural disasters (e.g., tornado, hurricanes, floods, etc.) are becoming increasingly familiar events that impact our college communities in unexpected and profound ways.

A survey of the literature on college crisis management suggests a variety of models and procedures have been developed to address many of these critical incidents on campus including: student deaths (Swenson & Ginsberg, 1996; Scott, Fukuyama, Dunkel & Griffin, 1992; Halberg, 1986); suicide (Mitchell, Elmore, & Fygetakis, 1996; Siegel, 1994); murders (Archer, 1992; Siegel, 1994); sexual assault (Siegel, 1994); and natural disasters (Siegel, 1994).

Siegel (1994) in her comprehensive review, *Campuses Respond to Violent Tragedy*, emphasizes the importance of colleges and universities learning from each other's crisis response efforts:

> I have seen that colleges and universities throughout the nation are struggling alone as they respond to campus violence. Since the tragic events discussed here can happen anywhere, I believe that institutional leaders will profit from understanding how their colleagues responded and how they reflected on their experiences (p. xi).

Anyone who has experienced a "critical incident," or has been on the front lines of responding knows that crises are "turning point events" that have the capacity to "overwhelm the usually effective coping skills of either an individual or group" (Mitchell & Everly, 1997, p. 6). Crises by their very nature occur when we are least expecting them and therefore our capacity to intervene effectively depends on our readiness. Swenson and Ginsberg (1996) have suggested that a model crisis intervention plan anticipates chaos and confusion while defining the specific actions that are designed to contain and lessen the impact.

Preparedness is of primary importance for those of us who—because of our professional roles and responsibilities—are called upon to plan for and attend to campus crises. Questions seldom considered by university administrators but that demand answers include:

- How ready are we as an institution to respond to critical incidents on campus?
- What protocols, resources, and personnel do we have in place?
- How quickly can we respond?
- How have our crisis responders been trained?
- What are the professional qualifications and experience of the responders?
- What approaches to crisis management are utilized?
- Who coordinates the crisis response?
- How does communication occur?
- What professional support is given to those who respond to critical incidents? (Who responds to the responders?)
- What protocol is used when the responders have been impacted by the crisis so that they are unable or ineffective at responding?

Experience in college crisis management has shown that these questions are best considered, policies and procedures developed, and trained personnel in place before critical incidents occur (see Chapter 7,

Pre-Crisis College Response). The importance of pre-crisis planning is clear and the costs more obvious; failure to prepare for campus crises jeopardizes a college's most valuable asset—the health and well being of its students, faculty, and staff.

This is the story of how one small liberal arts college in Southern Minnesota responded to a devastating tornado that nearly destroyed its campus in the spring of 1998. It highlights in a dramatic way the fundamentally important issues of pre-crisis planning.

The Tornado

It was spring break at Gustavus Adolphus College—a small liberal arts college of 2,350 students, perched at the top of a hillside overlooking the quaint town of St. Peter on the Minnesota River. Fortunately, the vast majority of students, faculty, and staff had left campus two days earlier, after the completion of midterm exams. However, a small number of students remained on campus, as well as a handful of faculty and staff who were working in buildings late Sunday afternoon on March 29, 1998.

Until the early evening it had been a beautiful, unusually warm spring day in St. Peter. The city's emergency management director just that morning had prepared radio public service announcements for the annual Severe Weather and Tornado Awareness Week, but that was still three weeks away (Rosario, 1999). A St. Peter police officer and trained weather spotter was on patrol three miles southwest of town when he pulled over on a gravel township road to get a better look at the darkening sky on the western horizon when a family van passed him on its way into town (Rosario, 1999). The weather was beginning to change rapidly. The sky suddenly darkened. Fierce rain, hail, and powerful wind closed in on the area and on the officer as he retreated into his squad car. "Sound the alarm again! I'm in the middle of it!" was the last transmission heard over the radio by the dispatcher before the tornado hit (Rosario, 1999). The family van that had passed the officer just moments before the funnel hit was carrying a 6-year-old boy who was thrown from the vehicle and injured fatally. The officer performed cardiopulmonary resuscitation on the boy en route to the hospital but was unsuccessful (Rosario, 1999).

Damage from the tornado was widespread and utterly horrifying. The six-year-old boy was killed and 30 others were injured. A fire gutted a building in downtown St. Peter, two historical churches were destroyed, and numerous historical structures were severely damaged or destroyed.

By a vote of 131-0, the Minnesota House of Representatives approved a $27.6 million bill to provide relief to victims of the tornado. The bill was approved in the Senate and immediately signed by the governor. It was reported in December 1998 that the tornado caused the demolition of 110 single-family structures, 44 rental properties and 23 commercial buildings. Forty-six lots were still vacant at the end of 1998, including 38 residential and eight commercial properties ("The devastating blow of 1998," 1999).

The college sitting on the top of a hill overlooking the town of St. Peter was a easy target for a fast moving tornado, as were many of the nearby homes of faculty and staff. Within an instant the 240-mph wind changed the landscape of the historic college forever. The 137-foot spire atop Christ Chapel in the center of campus was toppled, leaving a gaping hole in the roof where rain steadily poured down onto the pews and hymnals. Despite exposure to the elements, the eternal flame, suspended in a bowl from the ceiling of the chapel remained burning during the worst of the storm. The flame became a symbol for the resolve of the community to keep hope alive in desperate times.

The devastation on campus was widespread. Nearly every building on campus sustained significant damage. The residence halls were hit particularly hard with windows blown out and students' personal effects scattered randomly. An historic brick building that was home to a number of international students, many of whom were on campus when the tornado hit, sustained irreparable damage and needed to be taken down. Two other student houses on campus were completely leveled. All that remained was splintered wood that once made sturdy walls and piles of debris strewn over lawns and streets.

Windows were blown out, roofs were torn off buildings, and hundreds of cars were twisted and overturned in campus parking lots. Chain saws hummed and front-end loaders fed wood chippers for 10 days straight, 24 hours a day, grinding up over 2,000 trees. The total cost in damages for the college was estimated between $40 to $60 million dollars.

Damage and loss of buildings is unfortunate and costly; damage and loss of the human spirit is more severe and less easy to replace. We were fortunate that no one died or was seriously injured on our campus as a result of the tornado. However, there was a more subtle kind of loss that occurred with survivors of the tornado that was perhaps less tangible but more and more evident as the days of recovery dragged on. These were the individuals—students, faculty, and staff—who sustained significant personal loss and toward whom the crisis response effort was aimed. Through an examination of our institutional crisis response, we can learn much about what went well and what could have been done better.

Tornado Crisis Response

At the time of the tornado, I lived 70 miles north of St. Peter. The voice of my colleague on the other end of the phone was noticeably shaken as she described her personal reactions to the destruction that had just taken place on campus. "It's bad. . . its really bad. . . you would not believe the damage. . ." she said in a stunned tone.

A group of 50 to 100 students and staff were gathered in the safety of the athletic complex on campus. Safety and security officers, residential life staff, and my colleagues had a list of students who were staying on campus over spring break and they were trying to match names with those present. They accounted for all the students and settled in for what would be the first of many long, sleepless nights. We agreed to talk the next day to begin making plans for the recovery efforts.

Upon arriving on campus, accompanied by another psychologist who also worked in the counseling center, we were astounded at the physical destruction but even more concerned about the havoc the tornado had wrecked on our friends and colleagues at the college. Administrators, faculty, and staff were walking around campus in the rain with glazed looks on their faces trying to help out where they were needed. Many people whose homes were severely damaged or destroyed were attending to their families and trying to take inventory of what they had lost.

Signs that a recovery effort had started were apparent. The campus disaster plan had immediately been initiated and outside teams were brought in to assist in the clean up of buildings and the removal of debris. There was a general sense of anxiety and uncertainty about a number of important issues:

- How to communicate important information both internally on campus and externally to students who were still away on spring break?
- What exactly had been damaged or destroyed?
- When or if classes would resume?
- How could employees in various departments help each other out?
- What were the main priorities in terms of tasks needing to be done to assist with the recovery?

My area of responsibility initially was attending to the international students who had been on campus during the tornado and were now living off campus in the dorms at a state university. Having experience and background in Critical Incident Stress Management (CISM) in a college setting was useful in my crisis intervention work with our international students and also in terms of how I began to conceptualize our overall crisis response efforts. After several debriefings with students it was clear to me that they were, for the most part, doing fairly well. It was the administrators, faculty, and staff that I became more concerned about as time went on and the full impact of the tornado became more apparent. A decision was made by the administration and board of trustees to have students return to campus and resume classes on Tuesday, April 21, 1998—just 23 days after the tornado nearly destroyed the campus. The goal of reopening the campus had been set and the employees and alumni of the college continued to work at a feverish pace to meet this objective.

Crisis Intervention

The crisis interventions discussed in this chapter are explained in much greater detail in Dan Casey's chapters on the core components of CISM, pre-crisis planning, and CISM response on campus. Russell Lee's chapter on working with parents identifies the needs and interventions best used for that group.

CISM would have been extremely helpful for the employees of the college immediately following the tornado and in the days after the crisis response was in full swing. However, the time to convince a college administration that CISM is an effective intervention strategy is not after a critical incident has occurred. The level of disorientation and confusion after the tornado did not make an ideal environment for considering a new idea or approach to crisis intervention like CISM, no matter how effective it may be. I began to focus my attention on a priority that everyone could agree on—the well being of our students who would be returning to campus.

In the days following the tornado, my colleagues and I at the counseling center began calling other counseling center directors from around the state to request their assistance on our campus. We asked psychologists from other schools to be a presence on campus for our faculty and staff, not to provide debriefings for reasons already mentioned, although this would have been useful, but to walk around and talk to employees and alumni of the college who were assisting with the clean up. As I look back on this request now, with the perspective of Minnesota Inter-College Crisis Network (MICCN), its even more apparent to me that what our colleagues from other schools should have been doing is CISM. However, two years ago MICCN was just starting up, and the psychologists who generously donated their time did not know the procedures of CISM.

In addition to being an empathic presence to our crisis workers on campus, we asked these psychologists to return to campus to actually do Critical Incident Stress Debriefing (CISD) when the students returned. The college had reconstructed an academic schedule and made plans for post-tornado orientation sessions for all students prior to the start of classes. Student debriefings were planned out of concern about the level of loss that students may have experienced and the shock of adjusting to campus 23 days after the tornado.

To assist in these student-debriefing efforts, I contacted Dan Casey, an ICISF certified trainer, to request that his student-lead college CISM team assist us on campus. I had been consulting with Casey from the beginning of our crisis response and he felt confident that his trained student facilitators could be extremely effective debriefing our students. The plan included Casey's team arriving on campus a few hours before the student debriefings were scheduled so that his students could get oriented to our situation and the specific needs of the debriefings.

Joining Casey's team was a group of local psychotherapists, three psychologists from our counseling center, and our chaplain, as well as a small number of Gustavus student affairs professionals with group facilitation experience. The counseling center advertised the voluntary debriefings to students through the residence halls and offered different times that they could participate. Casey gave an overview and short training of the CISD model to the assemble professionals, most of whom had no prior experience with CISD, with the emphatic statement that they (the mental health professionals) must allow the trained CISM student team members to lead the debriefings. Approximately 80 students participated in the debriefings, with positive outcomes from each of the groups being reported in the post-debriefing discussion. It was generally thought that the student-trained debriefers on Casey's team provided the Gustavus student participants with a comfort level that might not otherwise be present with older adult facilitators.

The Development of MICCN

In addition to the tornado case study, I include in this review one of the many outcomes that has occurred as a direct result of the tornado. Taking seriously Siegel's (1994) suggestion that universities learn from each others crisis response models, a unique and important effort by Minnesota college counseling centers has developed to form a consortium of crisis responders who are trained to assist one another's campuses in the wake of large scale crises. MICCN is a network of colleges and universities across the state that have organized a cooperative crisis management team for the purpose of sharing resources, training, and assistance in times of need.

Inspired by the lessons learned from the Gustavus Adolphus College tornado recovery effort, St. Mary's College multiple student deaths, and Augsburg College's death of students, MICCN has developed into a valid resource for participating institutions in Minnesota. It is a guide for other educational institutions that share geographical proximity and similar goals regarding crisis response and the value of collaborative working relationships. The story of MICCN, and its organizational structure is presented for the purpose of providing guidelines to other colleges who may want to pursue the development of a similar consortium.

MICCN consists of a number of private and public colleges and universities in the state that have received training in the International Critical Incident Stress Foundation (ICISF) model of crisis intervention. Each of the colleges is registered with the ICISF and has developed a crisis intervention team on campus. Each serves its own people as needed and necessary. The number of interventions varies from college to college but averages approximately seven calls for each per year. The strength of the MICCN program lies in the development of its contact line. Any of the member colleges or universities that have a crisis incident which overwhelms or personally involves a number of their team can call one telephone number which will activate up to 60 CISM trained crisis interveners from across the state to address the crisis.

These activated groups will provide critical incident stress debriefings, defusings, or crisis management briefings. They will also provide one-on-one crisis intervention as necessary.

These visiting CISM teams will provide the interventions, while the home CISM team, knowing the campus and individuals very thoroughly, will do the assessment and planning, and will develop and guide the protocol necessary for the crisis interventions to happen.

MICCN has activated for death of a student, suicide, death of a professor, tornados, multiple death accidents, and a number of other incidents, including shutting down a major program that affected the entire campus.

Epilogue

In the period of recovery since the tornado, it has become clear that those of us who lived through this crisis are still processing the impact of what occurred both individually and collectively as a college community. In many ways our loss has become our gain. We continue our campaign to "Rebuild A Greater Gustavus." Buildings have been rebuilt, trees have been replanted, and academic life on the college moves on. However, there remain many reminders of our traumatic past. There are conversations at lunchtime about "the storm," we have memories of buildings and homes that are no longer standing, and I look around and see the tired look on my colleagues faces as they come to the end of another academic year. The debris may be gone but the individual and collective stress of the tornado remains. The unforeseen events of March 29, 1998, have left an indelible mark on our souls in powerful ways that exist to this day.

As a counseling center psychologist and frontline responder in the tornado recovery effort on campus, I continue to reflect upon and learn about what went well in our crisis response, and perhaps more importantly, what we as an institution, division of student affairs, and counseling center could have done differently. I do not mean to suggest that we responded poorly. On the contrary, there are countless examples of professionals who exceeded expectations in terms of what they did to assist in the recovery efforts. However, in the wake of this tragedy I continue to look for ways to make sense out of what happened, to reflect on our response efforts, and to summarize the lessons that we as an institution learned. It is these points of wisdom and experience that I hope have been conveyed in this review.

Nothing can really prepare someone for a crisis—be it a tornado or suicide attempt by a student in one of the dorms. Responding to critical incidents on campus has become an all too familiar part of what I do as a counseling center psychologist. At the end of the day, I am thankful for my training in CISM, for my colleagues who do similar work at other institutions, and for the support of one another that we are developing as the result of our professional responsibilities.

References

Archer, J. (1992). Campus in crisis: Coping with fear and panic related to serial murders, *Journal of Counseling and Development, 71,* 96-100.

The devastating blow of 1998. (1999, March 25). *The Saint Peter Herald,* p. 3.

Halberg, L. J. (1986). Death of a college student: Response by student services professionals on one campus, *Journal of Counseling and Development, 64,* 411-412.

Mitchell, S. L. , Elmore, K. , & Fygetakis, L.M. (1996). "A coordinated campus response to student suicide." *Journal of College Student Development, 37,* 698-699.

Mitchell, J. T., & Everly, G. S., Jr. (1997). Critical Incident Stress Debriefing: An Operations Manual for the Prevention of Traumatic Stress Among Emergency Services and Disaster Workers (2nd ed. rev.). Ellicott City, MD: Chevron Publishing.

Rosario, R. (1999, April 19). When storms gather, eyes on sky save lives. *Saint Paul Pioneer Press,* pp. B1, B3.

Scott, J. E., Fukuyama, M. A. , Dunkel, N. W. , & Griffin, W. D. (1992). The trauma response team: Preparing staff to respond to student death, *National Association of Student Affairs Administrators Journal, 29,* 230-237.

Siegel, D. (1994). Campuses respond to violent tragedy. Phoenix, AZ: *The Oryx Press.*

Swenson, D. X. , & Ginsberg, M. H. (1996). A comprehensive model for campus death postvention. *Journal of College Student Development, 37,* 543-549.

CHAPTER 2

Traumatic Stress Disorders

By Russell Lee, Ed.D.

Following exposure to sufficient trauma, it is normal to experience a variety of symptoms: fear, anger, physical problems, trouble concentrating, even numbness. Elsewhere in this book descriptions are given about how psychologists dealing with victims of trauma may "normalize," or let people know that some symptoms following trauma are to be expected. This chapter is about trauma symptoms and other responses that go beyond the normal, so that psychological disorders develop.

While stress itself is inevitable, sometimes even desirable, traumatic stress is defined by the *Diagnostic and Statistical Manual of Mental Disorders*, (DSM-IV-TR, American Psychiatric Association, 2000) as an event that involves at least the threat of death or serious injury to self or others and that creates intense feelings of fear, helplessness, or horror. Campus examples of traumatic stressors may include physical and sexual assaults, serious car accidents, suicides, homicides, natural disasters, and even campus shootings. All of these may cause serious injury, and many of them death or the threat of death. Witnesses and survivors both may experience a great deal of stress following exposure to these sorts of incidents. For some, the symptoms begin to fade after a few weeks. For others, the trauma continues for a much longer period of time.

Much of our early knowledge of traumatic stress disorders came from the military, war being a very stressful experience for combat troops, with early labels like "combat fatigue" and "shell shock" (Frances, First, & Pincus, 1995). The earliest definitions of stress disorders defined trauma as "outside the range of usual human experience," but we now know that exposure to trauma is a fairly common part of the human experience, and revisions attempted to define trauma more exactly (Frances et al., 1995). Yehuda (2002) estimates that as many as 35% of people exposed to an event as stressful as the destruction of the World Trade Center may develop significant symptoms of a stress disorder. Shmotkin, Blumstein, and Modan (2003) suggest that the effects of extreme stress, such as that experienced by holocaust survivors, can last for more than 60 years.

College and university campuses are not immune from traumatic events, including natural disasters and sexual assaults. These events can happen to students already stressed by the pressures of school, exams, and assignments. Nolen-Hoeksema (2004) says that natural disasters such as fires, floods, earthquakes, tornados, and hurricanes can "trigger a wave" of posttraumatic stress disorders among the people who survive them. Most survivors of sexual assault experience posttraumatic stress symptoms, and perhaps 25% still suffer from posttraumatic stress disorder several years after the assault (Foa & Riggs, 1995). Students sexually assaulted while in college may have the negative effects of that assault last throughout their college experience.

Warning Signs of Trauma Related Stress

Individuals who have experienced a traumatic event frequently suffer psychological stress related to the incident. Most often these are normal reactions to abnormal situations. People who feel they are unable to regain control of their lives or who experience the following symptoms for more than a month should seek psychological assistance. Many of the following symptoms are normal reactions to trauma related stress, but having many of the symptoms or having them for a prolonged period of time presents problems:

- Recurring thoughts or nightmares about the event.
- Having trouble sleeping or changes in appetite.
- Experiencing anxiety and fear, especially when exposed to events or situations reminiscent of the trauma.
- Being on edge, being easily startled, or becoming overly alert.
- Feeling depressed, sad, and having low energy.
- Experiencing memory problems including difficulty in remembering aspects of the trauma.

- Feeling "scattered" and unable to focus on work or daily activities.
- Having difficulty making decisions.
- Feeling irritable, easily agitated, or angry and resentful.
- Feeling emotionally "numb," withdrawn, disconnected, or different from others.
- Spontaneously crying, feeling a sense of despair and hopelessness.
- Feeling extremely protective of, or fearful for, the safety of loved ones.
- Not being able to face certain aspects of the trauma, and avoiding activities, places, or even people that remind you of the event. (Warning Signs of Trauma Related Stress, APA Fact Sheet. Retrieved March 2003, www.apa.org/practice/ptsd.html).

Traumatic Stress Disorders

Acute Stress Disorder (ASD) occurs within one month of exposure to the stressor and lasts, by DSM-IV-TR definition, not more than 4 weeks following the trauma. Several symptoms predominate: reexperiencing of the event (via dreams or daydreams, flashbacks, and intrusive thoughts), avoidance of reminders of the trauma (such as avoiding the dorm where the sexual assault took place), marked arousal or anxiety, and dissociative symptoms. Dissociative symptoms represent an attempt to separate from the trauma and from related events. People may become emotionally unresponsive and find it difficult to experience pleasure. They may have trouble with concentration, have difficulty recalling details about the traumatic event, and may even feel a sort of detachment from their bodies, experiencing the world in a surrealistic dream-like state. Although acute stress disorder is defined as lasting less than four weeks and many people recover within that period of time, people with these symptoms often go on to develop posttraumatic stress disorder right away, (Bryant & Harvey, 2000) and are at a high risk to develop posttraumatic stress disorder for months following the exposure to traumatic stress (Classen, Koopman, Hales, & Spiegel, 1998). Even people who do not quite meet the diagnostic requirements for ASD are more likely to develop posttraumatic stress disorder than are people with the same level of stress exposure but fewer symptoms (Harvey & Bryant, 1999).

ASD is a newer disorder than posttraumatic stress disorder, having first been included in DSM-IV in 1994 (American Psychiatric Association, 1994) with the intention of making treatment available to people exposed to traumatic stress before they developed posttraumatic stress disorder, in the hope that effective early treatment would prevent them from developing it (Frances et al., 1995). Many of the techniques discussed elsewhere in this book are designed to reduce the likelihood of progress from ASD to posttraumatic stress disorder.

Posttraumatic Stress Disorder (PTSD) has a similar cluster of symptoms as acute stress disorder, ranging from mild to immobilizing, but the effect tends to be long lasting. About 20 percent of women and 8 percent of men exposed to trauma will suffer from posttraumatic stress disorder at some time in their lives (Kessler, Sonnega, Bromet, Hughes, & Nelson, 1995). The greater percentage of women may be accounted for in part because women are far more likely to be sexually assaulted. The more severe the trauma, the more likely those exposed to it will develop the disorder.

The American Psychiatric Association (2000) specifies the criteria for PSTD in its *Diagnostic and Statistic Manual of Mental Disorders* (Table 2-1). This extensive symptom list is condensed in Table 2-2 into symptom clusters illustrated by examples.

Posttraumatic stress disorder is one of the few disorders for which we know the immediate cause. PTSD can result from exposure to extremely traumatic and stressful situations outside the realm of everyday human experience, yet common enough for many people to have experienced them. Such traumas include war, sexual assault, child abuse, severe accidents, and natural disasters. Yet not everyone exposed to a traumatic event will develop PTSD. Both genetic and environmental influences can play a role (Stein, Jang, Taylor, Vernon, & Livesley, 1993). The following case illustrates some of the difficulties of this disorder:

Krista and her three roommates lived off campus a block or so...close enough to walk to classes and less expensive than living in the residence halls because the four of then could split the rent for the crowded one bedroom apartment. Krista and Jane slept on single beds in the bedroom while Marcy and Bob shared the pullout couch in the living room.

Krista had never felt at risk in her apartment because it was so full of people. Given the single shared bathroom, the presence of Bob, and the frequent presence of Sam, Jane's boyfriend, and Jim, her own boyfriend, Krista got used to the reduction in modesty such living conditions required.

Table 2-1
APA Diagnostic Criteria for Posttraumatic Stress Disorder

A. The person has been exposed to a traumatic event in which both of the following were present:	1. The person experienced, witnessed, or was confronted with an event or events that involved actual or threatened death or serious injury, or a threat to the physical integrity of self or others. 2. The person's response involved intense fear, helplessness or horror. Note: In children, this may be expressed instead by disorganized or agitated behavior.
B. The traumatic event is persistently re-experienced in one (or more) of the following ways:	1. Recurrent and intrusive distressing recollections of the event, including images, thoughts, or perceptions. Note: In young children, repetitive play may occur in which themes or aspects of the trauma are expressed. 2. Recurrent distressing dreams of the event. Note: In children, there may be frightening dreams without recognizable content. 3. Acting or feeling as if the traumatic event were recurring (includes a sense of reliving the experience, illusions, hallucinations, and dissociative flashback episodes, including those that occur on awakening or when intoxicated). Note: In young children, trauma-specific reenactment may occur. 4. Intense psychological distress at exposure to internal or external cues that symbolize or resemble an aspect of the traumatic event. 5. Physiological reactivity on exposure to internal or external cues that symbolize or resemble an aspect of the traumatic event.
C. Persistent avoidance of stimuli associated with the trauma and numbing of general responsiveness (not present before the trauma), as indicated by three (or more) of the following:	1. Efforts to avoid thoughts, feelings or conversations associated with the trauma. 2. Efforts to avoid activities, places, or people that arouse recollections of the trauma 3. Inability to recall an important aspect of the trauma. 4. Markedly diminished interest or participation in significant activities. 5. Feeling of detachment or estrangement from others. 6. Restricted range of affect (e.g., unable to have loving feelings 7. Sense of foreshortened future (e.g., does not expect to have a career, marriage, children, or a normal life-span)
D. Persistent symptoms of increased arousal (not present before the trauma), as indicated by two (or more) of the the of the following:	1. Difficulty falling or staying asleep 2. Irritability or outbursts of anger 3. Difficulty concentrating 4. Hypervigilance 5. Exaggerated startle response
E. Duration of the disturbance (symptoms in Criteria B, C, and D) is more than 1 month.	
F. The disturbance causes clinically significant distress or impairment in social, occupational, or other important area of functioning.	

Table 2-2
Symptom Clusters for Posttraumatic Stress Disorder

Reexperiencing of the traumatic event	A student of mine was severely injured in an auto accident. It took months for her physical recovery, but longer for her to be able to drive. She had frequent nightmares about the accident, which happened in the right-hand lane of a two-lane highway. When she did begin to drive again, she was troubled by vivid images of the accident, which would cause her to swerve to the left, endangering oncoming traffic, in order to escape the imagined car coming towards her in her own lane. Near misses with oncoming traffic would cause her to pull off the road petrified with far, and she sometimes called a friend on her cell phone to get a ride back home.
Emotional numbing and detachment	Following the tornado that destroyed the house he was living in and all of his property, and that killed his only brother, Paul began to do what he called "reassessing his life." His internal focus was so involving that he no longer cared to spend time with his friends. He began drinking to excess, stopped going to his college classes, and spent a great deal of time playing computer video games. His feelings were generally restricted, except for guilt over the death of his brother, and he reported that he really had no friends any more. Asked about the future, he said that he could barely imagine tomorrow.
Hypervigilance and chronic arousal	During the Vietnam war, I headed a psychological testing unit for the Army and worked with a soldier who had recently returned from in country. We used a timer, which this soldier set, to record timed tests. Whenever the timer bell rang, the soldier would dive under the table, then sheepishly arise again. Because of his chronic hyper-vigilance, the timer startled him every time. He reported chronic difficulties with falling asleep.

One Wednesday night shortly before her graduation, an impromptu party was held at the apartment. Krista did not participate much, because she had a final exam the next day and wanted to go to sleep early. Her friends, all but Sam, who said he had drunk too much, went out. Krista went to bed, only to wake up an hour later to find her nightgown pushed up and Sam's weight pressing down on her. He was a big man, and his body pressed the air out of her. "I've always wanted you," he slurred. She felt him penetrate her and tried to push him off, but he continued to press her down, covering her face with kisses as he quickly came. Rolling off, he wordlessly dressed and left the apartment.

Krista felt shocked and devastated, but she also felt awkward and somehow responsible. She was afraid that Jane would think that she seduced Sam, and was even more afraid of what Jim would think if he found out that she and Sam had had sex. She wished that it had just never happened. Krista showered for a long time, and resolved to tell no one. Fortunately, Sam stopped coming by the apartment after the rape. Except for difficulty falling asleep for a few weeks and a certain amount of distractibility, Krista seemed OK.

Over the summer, Krista and Jim broke up. She did not feel as close to him as she once had, and he complained that she had become distant and uncaring. When she went to graduate school in the fall, Krista got a single room in the graduate dorm. As the pressures of graduate study built up, Krista began to feel more and more stressed. She would wake up terrified several times a night, sometimes from nightmares of the assault, and her loss of sleep seemed to reduce her ability to concentrate in classes. She formed few friendships, none with men, and did not date at all. As the school year neared its end, and the anniversary of her sexual assault approached, Krista became more and more distressed. She would picture the assault over and over in her mind, obsessing over it and trying to come up with ways she could have changed the outcome. She dropped out of school and sought therapy, but it was more than a year before she could resume classes again.

Krista, like many people who have experienced a traumatic event, reexperienced the event in different ways, by thinking about it over and over, by visualizing it, and by having nightmares about it. Some victims of PTSD have flashbacks: startling, realistic visual images, or auditory experiences as if the event was happening all over again. Reexperiencing an event might be expected to desensitize a person to it, but because the reexperiencing is accompanied by emotional arousal and physical discomfort, the effect is to re-traumatize the person over and over. Rarely, the reexperiencing occurs in a dissociative state, in which the person may think that the event actually is happening again (Oltmanns & Emery, 2004).

Krista also demonstrated emotional numbing and detachment. Victims of trauma may try to repress memories of the event. Krista wanted the assault to just have not happened, and she did not deal with it right away. In numbing her feelings about the event, she also numbed her feelings about others, including her boyfriend. These symptoms also tend to perpetuate the disorder. By distancing herself from her friends and her boyfriend, Krista lost a potential source of support and understanding. Her detachment cost her some of the joy of life, and thus made her vulnerable to a return of the feelings she had numbed herself against. When such unpleasant feelings return, as they might around the time of the anniversary of an event, the person can be shocked to find that they have not fully recovered as they thought they had, and that they now have to face these memories and feelings in a state perhaps more vulnerable than they were at first. Hypervigilance and chronic arousal were related to Krista's sleep difficulties. She had difficulty relaxing enough to sleep well, and her lack of sleep added further to her vulnerability. In the absence of treatment, Krista might have experienced PTSD for years. While Krista could not have prevented the assault, had she been able to process the event immediately after its occurrence and seek the emotional support of others, she might have suffered from acute stress disorder, but not have developed PTSD.

Once a person suffers from PTSD, attempts at relief, such as self-medicating with alcohol or other factors such as guilt and anxiety, can complicate recovery. Comorbidity with other disorders and other complications can develop in people with chronic PTSD, including the following:

- Alcohol and drug abuse or dependence
- Chronic anxiety
- Depression and increased risk for suicide
- Divorce and separation
- Unremitting guilt
- Low self-esteem
- Panic attacks
- Phobias
- Chronic unemployment (Breslau, Davis, Andreski, & Peterson, 1991; Kessler et al., 1995)

Such comorbidity factors need to be taken into account when planning treatment. Ouimette, Moos, and Finney (2003) found that when patients diagnosed with both substance use disorder and PTSD were given treatment for either substance use alone or substance use followed by immediate PTSD treatment, those who did not receive immediate PTSD treatment had a shorter period of remission.

Although we generally know what triggers PTSD, it is less clear why some persons walk away from these events with PTSD while others do not. One dimension is the severity and duration of the trauma. The longer the trauma lasts, and the more life threatening it is, the more likely its victims are to develop PTSD. Assault victims who were repeatedly and violently raped over a long period are more likely to develop PTSD than those whose assaults were shorter and less violent (Kilpatrick, Saunders, Amick-McMullan, Best, Vernon, & Resnick, 1989; Merrill, Thompson, Sinclair, Gold, & Milner, 2001). The importance of both genetic and situational factors is supported by Goldberg, True, Eisen, and Henderson (1990), who compared twins who served during the war in Vietnam. Monozygotic twins exposed to combat were more likely to develop PTSD concurrently than dizygotic twins. Yet when one monozygotic twin experienced risky combat situations, the other twin was also more likely to than was true of dizygotic twins.

Social support, absent for Krista in the case presented above, is helpful. Victims who have strong social support to help them discuss and process the traumatic event and its emotions are less likely to develop PTSD (King, King, Foy, Keane & Fairbank,1999). It appears that feeling in control while in the stressful situation lessens the likelihood that an individual will develop PTSD. Similarly, PTSD becomes more likely in persons who blame themselves and feel excessive guilt about the event. Some researchers believe that PTSD risk is raised in persons whose nervous systems are biologically more sensitive to the effects of stress. When these persons encounter a stressor they become more aroused and stay aroused longer, and thus the stressor has a greater impact on them than on the person who is biologically less vulnerable (van der Kolk, 1996; Yehuda, 2002).

Therapeutic Interventions For Traumatic Stress Disorders

Critical incident stress debriefings, defusings, and other forms of critical incident management, as discussed in a later chapter of this book are the early interventions of choice following exposure to traumatic stress. Ursano, Grieger, and McCarroll (1996) say that such interventions are designed to "metabolize" early stress symptoms so that they do not become chronic and crystallized. Once the symptoms of PTSD have been established, however, a more therapeutic and generally longer term intervention becomes necessary. Unfortunately, traditional psychotherapy has not been particularly useful for traumatic stress disorders. However, two techniques have been supported in the literature as being effective. See van Etten, & Taylor (1998) for a meta-analysis comparing efficacy of treatments for posttraumatic stress disorder.

Cognitive Behavior Therapy

Cognitive behavior therapy, and in particular, systematic desensitization, is an effective therapy for PTSD. In this form of therapy, the client is taught deep relaxation skills, and is asked to create a hierarchy of images related to the trauma, ranked from most anxiety provoking to least anxiety provoking. The client is asked to relax deeply, then starting with the least anxiety provoking, to imagine the images from their hierarchy. When the client indicates even a slight increase in anxiety, they are asked to let the image go, and to relax deeply again, paired with a relaxing image. The image is brought up again and again, paired with relaxation, until the client can visualize it with no anxiety at all. The client is then asked to visualize the next image in the hierarchy they constructed. By the time they can relax while visualizing the most anxiety provoking item on their list, their PTSD symptoms will have largely resolved. Krista, from the case presented earlier, would have been asked to create a list of images of the assault itself, and visualize it in detail.

Since the victim of PTSD probably already visualizes the critical incident over and over, via nightmares and flashbacks, how does systematic desensitization work? When the client visualizes the critical incident in an ordinary fashion, it is accompanied by intense negative feelings such as horror. The visualization victimizes the sufferer over and over. Using systematic desensitization the client feels no horror. At the first sign of anxiety, the image is replaced with relaxation and with a relaxing image. There is some evidence (Foa et al., 2002) that imaginal exposure can initially exacerbate PTSD symptoms, but not that this initial worsening has any clinical effect on either dropout rate or overall symptom reduction. The client learns to gain control, and is not re-victimized. This technique cannot be done mechanically, but rather needs to be done in an atmosphere of support and trust, by a caring and understanding therapist. The therapist needs to use other cognitive techniques as well, looking, for example, for distorted thinking patterns such as the unreasonable guilt felt by many victims of sexual assault. Stress management and help with managing one's feelings can be an important adjunct to this therapy (Wolfsdorf & Zlotnick, 2001). van Etten and Taylor (1998) report a number of studies supporting the effectiveness of these cognitive techniques.

Although usually the images are imagined, the procedure can be done *in vivo*, an effective but far less practical technique. A related cognitive-behavioral technique, *flooding*, involves keeping the client in the anxiety-provoking situation without paired relaxation, until the client eventually desensitizes because of prolonged exposure. A related therapy, cognitive-processing therapy (CPT), involves cognitive therapy focusing on distorted and over-generalized beliefs paired with exposure via writing and reading about the traumatic event, and has received some support in the literature (Resick, Nishith, Weaver, Astin, & Feuer, 2002).

Eye Movement Desensitization and Reprocessing

Eye movement desensitization and reprocessing (Shapiro, 1995) also involves repeated imaging of the stress inducing stimulus and attention to concurrent physical sensations, but during the imaging the therapist moves a finger back and forth in front of the client's eyes to stimulate a series of quick jerky eye movements similar to the rapid eye movements that occur during dreaming. Some therapists use light bars that flash, alternating spots on a wall, or other methods depending upon the needs of the client. The client rates their level of discomfort during the visualizing by using a scale called SUDS, or subjective units of distress, and the process is repeated until the client's SUDS ratings indicate a lowered anxiety level. The client also rates the validity of cognition (VOC) level as to positive cognition. This typically rises as the SUDS level declines. Early anecdotal success stories of this technique led to a large number of empirical studies (see Davidson & Parker, 2001, for a meta-analysis), many of which supported the effectiveness of the technique at reducing PTSD symptoms compared to no treatment wait lists or nonspecific treatments, and found EMDR to be about as effective as systematic desensitization. According to Parnell (1999) "At this point there are more controlled studies on EMDR showing significant treatment effects than on any other method used in the treatment of post-traumatic stress disorder."

Early advocates claimed that the technique could reduce PTSD symptoms in a single session, giving the technique a big advantage over systematic desensitization, but more recently advocates recommend multiple sessions (Resick & Calhoon, 2001). Davidson and Parker (2001) also looked at studies that compared EMDR with and without the eye movement itself, and concluded that the eye movement made no difference. Re-exposure and habituation thus appear to be the active mechanisms for both EMDR and systematic desensitization.

Medications

Medications have only recently been found effective for PTSD. The U.S. Food and Drug Administration approved the use of the antidepressant Zoloft in 1999 and Paxil in 2002. Oltmanns and Emery (2004) say that the success of these medications is likely because of the comorbidity between PTSD and depression. They note that traditional antianxiety medications are not effective for treating PTSD. When PTSD is accompanied by symptoms of depression, the use of antidepressant medication along with therapy would seem advisable.

Traumatic Stress Disorders

Traumatic stress disorders such as ASD and PTSD are the result of exposure to horrific stressors, especially those that threaten injury or death and that produce intense fear. Once thought to be outside the realm of normal human experience, we now know that such stressors are common, and that the college and university environment is not immune to them. Although the presence of symptoms following exposure to such stress is normal, given sufficient severity of the stressor or a social or biological predisposition the symptoms of exposure to stress can exacerbate to form traumatic stress disorders. PTSD can be a very long lasting and debilitating disorder. Fortunately it responds to treatment. It is important for those of us who work in the college and university environment to be aware of the symptoms of stress disorders so that we can refer the victims of stress to appropriate treatment.

References

American Psychiatric Association. (1994). *Diagnostic and statistical manual of mental disorders* (4th ed.). Washington, DC: Author.

American Psychiatric Association. (2000). *Diagnostic and statistical manual of mental disorders*. (DSM-IV-TR, 4th ed., text revision). Washington, DC: Author.

Breslau, N., Davis, G. C., Andreski, P., & Peterson, E. (1991). Traumatic events and posttraumatic stress disorder in an urban population of young adults. *Archives of General Psychiatry, 48,* 216-222.

Bryant, R.A., & Harvey, A.G. (2000). *Acute stress disorder: A handbook of theory, assessment and treatment*. Washington, DC: American Psychological Association.

Classen, C., Koopman, C., Hales, R., & Spiegel, D. (1998). Acute stress disorder as a predictor of posttraumatic stress symptoms. *American Journal of Psychiatry, 155,* 620-624.

Davidson, P. R., & Parker, K.C.H. (2001). Eye movement desensitization and reprocessing (EMDR): A meta-analysis. *Journal of Consulting & Clinical Psychology, 69,* 305-316.

Foa, E. B., & Riggs, D.S. (1995). Post-traumatic stress disorder following assault: Theoretical considerations and empirical findings. *Current Directions in Psychological Science, 4,* 61-65.

Foa, E.B., Zoellner, L.A., Feeny, N.C., Hembree, E. A., & Alvarez-Conrad, J. (2002). Does imaginal exposure exacerbate PTSD symptoms? *Journal of Consulting and Clinical Psychology, 70,* 1022-1028.

Frances, A., First, M.B., & Pincus, H.A. (1995). *DSM-IV guidebook*. Washington, DC: American Psychiatric Press.

Goldberg, J., True, W.R., Eisen, S.A., & Henderson, W.G. (1990). A twin study of the effects of the Vietnam War on posttraumatic stress disorder. *Journal of the American Medical Association, 263,* 2725-2729.

Harvey, A.G., & Bryant, R.A. (1999). The relationship between acute stress disorder and post-traumatic stress disorder: a 2-year prospective evaluation. *Journal of Consulting and Clinical Psychology, 67,* 985-988.

Kessler, R.C., Sonnega, A., Bromet, E., Hughes, M., & Nelson, C.B. (1995). Post-traumatic stress disorder in the National Comorbidity Survey. *Archives of General Psychiatry, 52,* 1048-1060.

Kilpatrick, D.G., Saunders, B.E., Amick-McMullan, A., Best, C.L., Vernon, L. J., & Resnick, H.S. (1989). Victim and crime factors associated with the development of crime-related post-traumatic stress disorder. *Behavior Therapy, 20,* 199-214.

King, D.W., King, L.A., Foy, D.W., Keane, T.M., & Fairbank, F.A. (1999). Post-traumatic stress disorder in a national sample of female and male Vietnam veterans: Risk factors, war-zone stressors, and resilience recovery variables. *Journal of Abnormal Psychology, 109,* 164-170.

Merrill, L.L. , Thompson, C.J., Sinclair, B.B., Gold, S.R., & Milner, J.S. (2001). Predicting the impact of child sexual abuse on women: The role of abuse severity, parental support, and coping strategies. *Journal of Consulting and Clinical Psychology, 69,* 992-1006.

Nolen-Hoeksema, S. (2004). *Abnormal psychology* (3rd ed.). McGraw Hill: Boston.

Oltmanns, T.F., & Emery, R.E. (2004). *Abnormal psychology* (4th ed.). Pearson Education: Upper Saddle River, NJ.

Ouimette, P., Moos, R.H., & Finney, J.W. (2003). PTSD treatment and 5-year remission among patients with substance use and posttraumatic stress disorders. *Journal of Consulting and Clinical Psychology, 71,* 410-414.

Parnell, L. (1999). *EMDR in the treatment of adults abused as children.* (p. 2). Norton: New York.

Resick, P.A., & Calhoon, K.S. (2001). Post-traumatic stress disorder. In D. H. Barlow (Ed.) *Clinical handbook of psychological disorders: A step-by-step treatment manual* (3rd ed., pp. 60-113). New York: Guildford Press.

Resick, P.A., Nishith, P., Weaver, T.L., Astin, M.C., & Feuer, C.A. (2002). A comparison of cognitive-processing therapy with prolonged exposure and a waiting condition for the treatment of chronic post-traumatic stress disorder in female rape victims. *Journal of Consulting and Clinical Psychology, 70,* 867-879.

Shapiro, F. (1995). *Eye movement desensitization and reprocessing.* New York: Guilford.

Shmotkin, D., Blumstein, T., & Modan, B. (2003). Tracing long-term effects of early trauma: A broad-scope view of holocaust survivors in late life. *Journal of Consulting and Clinical Psychology, 71,* 223-224.

Stein, M.B., Jang, K.L., Taylor, S., Vernon, P.A., & Livesley, W.J. (1993). Genetic and environmental influences on trauma exposure and posttraumatic stress disorder symptoms: A twin study. *American Journal of Psychiatry, 159,* 1675-1681.

Ursano, R. J., Grieger, T. A. & McCarroll, J. E. (1996). Prevention of post-traumatic stress: Consultation, training, and early treatment. In B.A. van der Kolk, A.C. McFarlane, & L. Weisaeth (Eds.) *Traumatic stress* (pp. 441-462). New York: Guilford.

van der Kolk, B.A. (1996). The psychobiology of PTSD. In B.A. van der Kolk, A.C., McFarlane, & L. Weisaeth (Eds.) *Traumatic Stress* (pp. 3-23). New York: Guilford.

van Etten, M., & Taylor, S. (1998). Comparative efficacy of treatments for posttraumatic stress disorder: A meta-analysis. *Clinical Psychology and Psychotherapy, 5,* 126-145.

Wolfsdorf, B.A., & Zlotnick, C. (2001). Affect management in group therapy for women with posttraumatic stress disorder and histories of childhood sexual abuse. *Journal of Clinical Psychology, 57,* 169-181.

Yehuda, R. (2002). Current concepts: Post-traumatic stress disorder. *New England Journal of Medicine, 346,* 108-114.

CHAPTER 3

Vicarious Traumatization

By Beth Doshan, B.A.

While there has been an abundance of literature supporting the existence and deleterious effects of Posttraumatic Stress Disorder (PTSD), it is only within the past decade that psychological literature recognizing the negative effects of secondary exposure to traumatic material has emerged.

We are now aware that the effects of trauma may be contagious. In the role of listener, the crisis worker becomes a witness to a traumatic incident or disaster, and may become emotionally overwhelmed by the nature of the events. As a result, the listener becomes a secondary victim to the traumatic experience of the primary victim and may experience similar symptoms as the primary victim. This appears to be a natural consequence of caring between the primary victim(s) and crisis workers. Professionals and trained volunteers, who listen to victim's stories of fear, pain and suffering, may experience similar pain, etc., as a result of caring. Figley (1995) describes this as "a member of the support network experiencing the effects of trauma following contact with primary victims."

Vicarious traumatization (vicarious trauma) refers to the impact of repeated exposure to traumatic client imagery and material. In the role of listener, a crisis worker may experience a contagion effect, and thus begin to have symptoms similar to those of the primary victim. The listener experiences, to some degree, the same rage, terror and despair as the traumatized person (Herman, 1997). Various literatures on the subject of vicarious traumatization support the theory that people can be traumatized without actually having been directly physically harmed or threatened.

Another term used to describe the phenomenon of vicarious trauma in crisis workers is "compassion fatigue," a concept that has emerged in professional literature in recent years. Compassion fatigue represents the cost of caring about and for traumatized people. It is the emotional residue of exposure to working with traumatized, suffering people (Figley, 1995). Compassion fatigue and vicarious trauma differ from "burnout," which is associated with the everyday type of stress that one encounters. Burnout is cumulative, relatively predictable, and is frequently remedied by distancing from the sources of stress (Maslach and Jackson, 1981). Vicarious trauma and burnout are similar in that they both result in a reduced sense of personal accomplishment, discouragement and feelings of inadequacy related to working with traumatized people. The difference between the two is that symptoms of vicarious trauma do not decrease by distancing from the stressor.

Vicarious trauma is also referred to as Secondary Traumatic Stress (STS). McCann and Pearlman (1990b); Pearlman and Saakvitne (1995) elaborate a conceptual framework of vicarious trauma distinguishing it from STS. They describe vicarious trauma in the context of its profound changes in one's sense of meaning, identity, worldview, and beliefs about self and others.

STS is a cluster of symptoms nearly identical to posttraumatic stress, except that the exposure to knowledge of the traumatic event experienced by the listener (crisis worker, therapist, significant others) is indirect (Figley, 1994). In both instances, the traumatized person has experienced an event or accumulation of events, considered to be outside the range of usual human experience that would be significantly distressing to most people.

A full description of the Diagnostic and Statistical Manual IV-Revised definition of posttraumatic stress disorder can be found in Chapter 2 on Traumatic Stress Disorders.

The lifetime prevalence rate of PTSD in community-based studies ranges from 1% to 14%, with the variability related to methods of ascertainment and the population sampled. Studies of at-risk individuals (e.g., combat veteran, victims of volcanic eruptions or criminal violence) have yielded prevalence rates ranging from 3% to 58%.

The DSM-IV-R further states that the severity, duration, and proximity of an individual's exposure to the traumatic event are the most important factors affecting the likelihood of developing this disorder. There is some evidence that social supports, family history, childhood experiences, personality variables, and pre-existing mental disorders may influence the development of PTSD. This disorder can develop in individuals without any predisposing conditions, particularly if the stressor is especially extreme. It has been suggested by some trauma experts that PTSD should stand for primary traumatic stress disorder, rather than posttraumatic stress disorder, since stress reactions, by definition, are "post" trauma (Figley, 1995).

Vicarious Trauma is not listed in the DSM IV-R; however, many individuals who have researched vicarious trauma have indicated that the symptoms of vicarious trauma are identical to PTSD. Differentiation lies in the causal factor. PTSD is the result of trauma directly experienced by the affected individual, whereas vicarious trauma is the result of (secondary) trauma indirectly experienced by an affected individual. For the crisis worker, vicarious trauma is often the result of listening to and caring for traumatized people, and from repetitive secondhand exposure to traumatic material.

History of the Diagnostic Labels

To understand the emergent recognition of vicarious trauma in crisis workers, one must delve into the history of emergence of posttraumatic stress disorder as a diagnostic label and the phenomenon of countertransference.

Figley (1995) suggests that vicarious trauma, which he refers to as *"Compassion Fatigue"*(CF), is identical to *Secondary Traumatic Stress* (STS) and is the equivalent of PTSD. Posttraumatic stress disorder is a term that was coined following the Vietnam War. Therapists who worked with Vietnam War veterans realized that this group of people suffered from symptoms directly related to what they had seen, heard, and otherwise experienced during active duty in Vietnam. Although the phenomenon was recognized following WWI, as "shell shock" and Kardiner's (1947) "[post] traumatic neurosis," and again following WWII as "survivor syndrome" (Krystal, 1968), the term PTSD was not formulated until later. Interestingly, some therapists who work with this population also describe experiencing similar symptoms themselves as a result of listening to stories and witnessing the emotional pain of their clients. It is this secondary contamination, experienced by the therapist, which we refer to as "vicarious trauma."

Countertransference may be described as a therapist's reaction to a client in the context of psychotherapy resulting from the therapist's distortions. It is the result of over-identifying with the client's issues and responding in a manner to meet the therapist's own needs. In the context of psychotherapy, it is a reaction by the therapist to transference actions of the client and as such, may be a negative consequence of therapy if it interferes with the therapist's ability to be objective. Countertransference is, however, a natural consequence of caring between the therapist and client, one of whom has been traumatized (client), and the other (therapist), who is affected by the (client's) relating of the traumatic events.

Hudnall-Stamm (National Center for PTSD, Work-Related Secondary Traumatic Stress, [abstract] 2001) believes that countertransference is a broader concept that refers to our reactions to our clients and their material. It may direct therapeutic choices and is a state condition tied directly to the patient. By contrast, CF/STS/vicarious trauma, which results from working with trauma victims, induces more trait-like changes to our values, beliefs, and behaviors. Countertransference may occur outside of the context of exposure to traumatic material. CF/STS/vicarious trauma always arises as a result of exposure to a client's traumatic material, and applies to how our clients affect our lives, our relationships with ourselves, our social networks, as well as our work.

Identifying Crisis Workers at Risk

The very same qualities that lead a person to venturing into the field of crisis work paradoxically increase the likelihood that this worker will be more vulnerable to experiencing vicarious trauma. Crisis workers who are empathic, compassionate, genuine, emotionally present, honest and resourceful, tend to be quite effective doing the type of work required of them in the crisis intervention and mental health fields. Due to their capacity for feeling and expressing empathy, they are more vulnerable to the effects of vicarious trauma. Emotional exhaustion resulting from the process of caring for traumatized others increases susceptibility to experiencing adverse reactions.

Persons who have previously experienced events similar to that of the traumatized person, or who, in some way, feel personally connected with some aspect of the event(s) may be more prone to traumatic symptoms. For example, crisis workers who have children may experience trauma symptoms as a result of working with traumatized children, or with a parent who has lost a child. Children's trauma is provocative for crisis workers. Emergency workers report that they feel most vulnerable to effects of secondary trauma when working with children in pain. Female crisis workers who work with rape victims or battered women may have feelings of vulnerability, anger and helplessness similar to those of the primary female victim. Crisis workers who debrief traumatized individuals in similar vocations may share the same emotions and symptoms as those who were directly affected.

It is not unusual for the crisis worker who has directly experienced a traumatic event in his/her own life to be triggered (i.e., traumatic memories reemerge) by a victim's telling of a similar event. If the crisis worker has not fully processed or resolved his/her own traumatic event, there is increased risk of experiencing trauma symptoms. Pearlman and MacIan's (1995) empirical study found that therapists with personal trauma histories reported more difficulties with client material than those without. Personal traumatic experiences are a common factor shared by individuals who pursue a vocation in the field of traumatology and crisis work. Experiential reference has pros and cons in relation to working in these fields. Personal experience with similar trauma often enhances characteristics of empathy and compassion, traits that are considered desirable for enhancing therapeutic rapport and effectiveness. Paradoxically, this same reference may increase the risk of being triggered by the victim's experiences, resulting in vicarious trauma for the crisis worker.

Clearly, there is evidence to support the fact that over-involvement and over-identification with traumatized individual's events and symptoms can be detrimental to the efficacy and health of the crisis worker. Valent (1995) and Figley (1995) suggest that over-identification with a client's traumatic material and ineffective coping strategies contribute to the development of symptoms associated with STS/vicarious trauma. Rainer (1983) notes that if the individual's needs are perceived by the caregiver to be beyond his personal or professional resources, then the probability of stress increases for the caregiver.

Pearlman and Saakvitne (1995) identified two major factors that contribute to vicarious trauma: aspects of work and aspects intrinsic to the individual therapist (i.e., crisis worker). Aspects of work, which were identified, include: the nature of clientele, specific facts of traumatic events, organizational contextual factors, and social/cultural issues. Additionally, for the crisis worker, the rate of responses to critical incidents seems to be a factor, as well as the issue of whether or not the worker debriefed the incidents to which he responded. Aspects intrinsic to the therapist refer to those characteristics of the therapist/crisis worker that include: personality, personal history, current personal circumstances, and level of professional development.

Other studies have further identified that the age of therapist, level of exposure to traumatic material, coping strategies, and locus of control impact the risk of vicarious trauma. Younger therapists were more likely to report increased exposure to critical incident stress, felt greater levels of perceived threat, and had lower scores of adjustment, identity, inhibition and prudence scales on the Hogan Personality Inventory while having higher scores on measures of coping by means of escape-avoidance, self control, and active problem solving and had greater externality of locus of control (Marmar, Weis, Metzler, & Delucci, 1996).

Still further, the following personality traits and vocational/organizational factors have been identified as contributing to increased risk of traumatization for crisis workers:

Personality traits — neuroticism, history of psychiatric symptoms, inadequate coping (i.e., searching for meaning, denial of impact), unrealistic self-expectations (i.e., trying to "save the world").

Organizational factors — widespread "macho attitude" that pervades the crisis worker culture, confidentiality, and "no talk" rule, lack of adequate training, second-job stress (i.e., crisis work as a voluntary job), lack of a support system or supportive relationships, and role orientation.

Personality traits such as neuroticism are often indicative of a dysfunctional coping style and a tendency to have difficulty dealing with stress and crisis in general. Psychiatric symptoms may be triggered by physical and/or emotional stress. Given that crisis work is generally stressful, this line of work may not be suitable for some individuals with certain psychiatric conditions or symptoms. Individuals who have difficulty maintaining emotional stability under stress may do more harm than good for their clients in crisis in addition to exacerbating their own symptoms.

Inadequate coping skills are sometimes the result of denying that the victim's rendition of the trauma has any impact on the listener. This strategy is a way of emotionally detaching from the traumatic event. Lewinski (ongoing seminar) refers to one's presentation of emotional invulnerability as "Super-Human Syndrome." Lewinski's research indicates that police officers who are often subjected to exposure of others' trauma may adopt this method of coping in order to avoid emotional involvement with the traumatic material. While this may appear to be an effective coping style short term, repetitive and continued detachment may decrease effectiveness in helping victims of trauma due to an unwillingness or inability to emotionally connect. Long term, this style of coping will take a toll on the crisis worker in other areas of his/her life. A tendency to emotionally "shut down" and thus disconnect from significant relationships may be the resultant effect.

Individuals who attempt to search for a rational meaning or reason for the trauma may find themselves prone to crossover thinking in which they blame the victim or identify with perpetrators of a crime-based trauma. Failure to attribute meaning and unrealistic self-expectations may lead to feelings of hopelessness, helplessness, inadequacy and despair. Trauma victims and crisis workers may concurrently experience these deleterious effects.

Certain organizational structures and prevailing attitudes within the organization may be detrimental to the health of the crisis worker and the organization as a whole. A prevailing attitude of "masochism" may result in denying emotional and/or physiological distress resulting from dealing with traumatic events. There is a tendency to minimize the event and/or people in the organization do not talk about the effects of the traumatic event. Organizations that are governed by confidentiality policies and laws leave workers with fewer options for venting and sharing information about traumatic material disclosed by clients in the course of therapy/treatment. Individuals within such an organization may perceive symptoms of vicarious trauma as a sign of weakness or inadequacy, in which case they may fail to solicit assistance when it is needed. An organizational structure that is unsupportive of caring for its members' mental health needs risks producing an overall reduction of efficacy and performance, discontentment, derision, and an increased use of sick leave and turnover.

Convincingly, the current research and ensuing literature demonstrates that concurrent factors may increase the risk of vicarious trauma in crisis workers. Yet, it remains unclear as to why some workers may experience more intense, frequent or prolonged effects than others possessing similar traits and levels of exposure. The study of resiliency factors requires further investigative research. Some workers cite a healthy spirituality and strong support system as coexisting factors contributing to resiliency. The role of spirituality in resiliency and recovery is now emerging in the medical health field, but remains relatively obscure in literature specific to the issue of mental health. McCann and Pearlman (1990b) describe the effects of vicarious trauma as having a cumulative and permanent effect on one's emotional and spiritual health due to significant disruptions in one's sense of meaning, connection, identity, world view and other aspects of psychological, cognitive, relational, and emotional self.

Persons who work with traumatized individuals are inevitably at risk of experiencing vicarious trauma at some point in their career. Repeated and/or prolonged exposure to others' traumatic experience has a contagious effect. This knowledge and awareness of personal risk factors goes far to mitigating the impact of vicarious trauma.

Etiology of Symptoms

In the process of caring for others we may become so emotionally exhausted that we begin to experience adverse reactions. Judith Herman (1997) describes how therapists experience, to a lesser degree, the same feelings of rage, terror, and despair as the traumatized individual. The listener of victims' stories may begin to experience symptoms of PTSD similarly to the victims', despite their best efforts to avoid mirroring the victims' responses to trauma. Herman adds that trauma is contagious. In the role of listener to the recantation of a traumatic event, one is acting as a witness to these events. The listener may become emotionally overwhelmed and experience symptoms of PTSD.

Repeated exposure to stories of human suffering inevitably challenges the core values and sense of mortality of the crisis worker. They may experience a change in perception and interactions with the world and those around them. For example, in working with female victims of rape, the crisis worker may begin to develop a distrust of all men. They may find themselves becoming increasingly cynical about the motives of others and pessimistic about the human condition.

The effects of vicarious trauma are unique to each crisis worker. As previously discussed, certain factors intrinsic to the crisis worker, level of exposure to traumatic material, organizational factors, availability and strength of support network, and relationship to the victim/trauma, interact to develop or prevent vicarious trauma symptoms. A traumatic incident or traumatic material that has a significant impact on one individual may have very little impact on another. Each person responds to stressors in their own way. The duration of recovery, significance, and number of symptoms varies across individuals, even those who experience the same/similar events.

Examples of traumatic events crisis workers are exposed to include, but are not limited to: conveying tragic news to family members or friends of victims; listening to recantations of rape, assault, suicide, accidental and violent death incidents; witnessing effects of property or environmental loss due to tornadoes, floods, earthquakes, hurricanes, and fire; being exposed to suboptimal or dangerous conditions in the course of work; or witnessing victim's grief and pain. Working with the aftermath of trauma involves more than just exposure to a traumatic event. It also involves exposure to the survivor's reactions and other societal or institutional responses that re-victimize the survivor, as in the case of working with rape victims who may have to relive the experience in the legal process.

General changes, which may initially be unrecognized as symptomatic of vicarious trauma, include having no time or energy for self or others, increased feelings of cynicism, sadness, seriousness, and stronger emotions of anger, grief, or despair. There may be an increased sensitivity to violence as well.

McCann and Pearlman (1990b) suggest that the deleterious effects of vicarious trauma intrude upon four major areas of functioning: cognitive schema, psychological needs, memory system, and frame of reference. The way one views the world, others, self, relationships, and spirituality may be permanently altered as a result of vicarious trauma. Repeated exposure to stories of human suffering inevitably challenges one's basic faith and heightens one's sense of vulnerability. Our mortality and the brevity of life are brought to the forefront. Intrusions in the aforementioned four areas also result in alterations in one's sense of identity and ability to maintain a positive sense of self and connect to others; in the ability to manage strong emotions; as well as one's basic needs for and concepts about safety, esteem, trust, control, and intimacy.

When one's frame of reference or basic assumptions are disrupted due to experiencing another's trauma, one begins to question his/her own identity. This seems to be a hallmark characteristic of vicarious trauma. A sense of oneself as confused, jaded, cynical, inadequate, or depleted may reflect a disruption in sense of identity.

One's core values and how we perceive the world will be challenged. For example, a belief that most people are good and adhere to a set of values, that the world or society in which we live is a safe and just place to be, or that most people have some control or influence over events and outcomes in their lives will be severely questioned. A cynical world view may emerge and acceptance of violence and trauma as inevitable is not uncommon. One may begin to view others as basically untrustworthy and uncaring. Ultimately, this also affects interpersonal relationships.

Over time, one may begin to lose hope, a sense of meaning to life, disconnect from others or relationships, and question the existence of God if they previously held the belief in a God. As one's spirituality erodes, it becomes even more difficult to attach to any sense of hope or meaning.

What factors, then, contribute to a crisis/trauma worker's level of risk or vulnerability to the effects of vicarious trauma? Trauma work places special demands upon the crisis worker. Trauma and crisis are painful realities in our world that we must acknowledge and accept if we are to help trauma survivors. In our acknowledgment, we are made aware of the potential for trauma in our own lives. The risk implied, in continuing our work, is that we may also experience the effects of vicarious trauma that will inevitably change our own lives.

For crisis workers who have already experienced traumatic events similar to those of the survivors they help, it is a reminder of the losses the worker may have already experienced. Having painful memories and emotions evoked may result in further undermining one's own abilities and professional identity, which is detrimental to the helping process.

Mitigating Impact

Many times crisis workers realize that something is different, or all is not well with them; however, they may be unaware of what that "something" is resulting from. This may be due to an unawareness of causal factors and/or denial of symptoms.

Denial of aspects of vicarious trauma hinders the healing process by prolonging and exacerbating emergent symptoms. Unfortunately, denial of vulnerability and risk, symptomatology, and impact are all too common in some helping professions, as previously mentioned in this chapter. Denial prevents one from seeking the help and support needed to begin the process of healing. The most important and frequently used remedies for those suffering vicarious trauma effects are usually personal rather than clinical. This includes the naturally occurring support of family, co-workers, and friends, who may not know how to help if one is in denial.

Awareness of the existence of and symptoms associated with vicarious trauma is perhaps an important first step towards mitigating the impact of the effects of vicarious trauma. Educating crisis and trauma workers, mental health professionals, and others in the support network provides these people with the awareness required to identify the symptoms and impact of vicarious trauma. It also promotes further exploration of effective supportive and treatment strategies to mitigate the effects of vicarious trauma, although it may not prevent its occurrence.

Debriefing crisis workers following a traumatic event helps establish a framework to allow for ventilation. It is a process through which those involved in helping victims of trauma may safely explore and piece together the chronological, cognitive, emotional, spiritual, and physiological responses experienced as a result of helping. The debriefing process sets up a supportive response network for crisis workers who may not otherwise seek support on their own.

Maintaining a balance in one's life is crucial to overall good mental and physical health. It is important to emphasize this with those in the helping professions who may have a tendency to immerse themselves in their work. A balance of work, rest, and play also helps one keep a healthy perspective. Interactions with others outside of the crisis work arena keep us connected to broader aspects of the world and others in our lives.

Identifying and actively using healing activities on a regular basis as a restorative and maintenance strategy help ameliorate effects of vicarious trauma and decrease the risk.

Case Histories

The following case histories, specific to the college setting, depict the triggering effects of listening to others' renditions of their own traumatic events:

Bob, a counselor in the Counseling Center of a small liberal arts college, lost his only son in a car accident. Bob was driving and escaped with minor injuries, but his son had been pinned in the car for some time until fire fighters had been able to free him. The boy's injuries were too severe for him to live. Bob worked through his grief over the loss of his son over a period of time, and eventually felt that he had come to terms with his loss.

Ten years later, Bob's college was hit by a tornado and suffered significant damage. Bob was out of the state at a convention at the time and came back two days later to find part of the campus in shambles. The building that housed the Counseling Center was unaffected, however, and Bob began to see clients who were bothered by the incident. One client described seeing a tree fall on a car and crush the driver inside the car. She described in heavily emotional detail what it was like to stand helplessly outside the vehicle while the driver suffered inside it.

After a while Bob found himself unable to listen to her story. The experience of his own car accident came flooding back to him in an intense flash back and interfered with his ability to concentrate. At the conclusion of the session, he felt unable to see additional clients and went home experiencing intense depression. He kept reexperiencing the death of his son over and over in his mind. Bob did not sleep well that night, and felt that he could not return to work in the morning.

If Bob continues to have these symptoms, he could be diagnosed with Posttraumatic Stress Disorder, Delayed, but what precipitated the symptoms was the vicarious trauma of listening to the emotional detail of his client's experience and Bob's vulnerability to this particular trauma story. As a counselor, Bob at first listened thoroughly and empathetically to his client's story. He had to, for it was his job. The client did not moderate her story to save Bob's feelings. She had no way of knowing of his vulnerability. As the client, she needed to express herself with intensity and openness.

While Bob's vicarious traumatization was due to his vulnerability because of a similar traumatic event earlier in his life, the presence of a similar earlier event is not necessary in order to experience vicarious traumatization, as the next case will demonstrate.

Mary, who worked in student housing at a large metropolitan university, was a member of her campus crisis team. She was called to an intervention following a violent sexual assault that took place in the residence halls. Working with a group of women residents, who were not directly involved with the assault or with the victim, but who had been deeply upset by the event and wished to talk about it, Mary heard story after story of sexual coercion and even date rape from the participants of the session. Although she had never experienced a sexual assault or the level of sexual coercion that these women had, their stories angered and upset her. She had always felt herself somehow safe from the possibility of sexual assault, thinking that that happened to other women, not to her. As she participated in the group discussion, though, she became more and more aware of her own vulnerability to assault. No debriefing was held for discussion facilitators following this intervention, and Mary went home upset.

Over the next couple of weeks, Mary became increasingly worried about the possibility of sexual assault, and although once she had been rather free-spirited, she began restricting her activities. She felt safer when she was with her boyfriend, but also increasingly angry at him for some of his masculine traits. She felt vulnerable when he was not around, but argued with him whenever he was. As their relationship deteriorated, she began to feel hopelessly trapped in a dependent relationship.

Mary's vicarious traumatization was not due to vulnerability because of an earlier sexual assault, but rather because as a woman she identified with the assault survivors, all of whom were also women. It is interesting to note that the participants of the intervention felt considerably better after the group discussion. They came to the session feeling badly and felt some catharsis via the discussion. Mary came to the session feeling fine, but was bothered by the stories she heard. Had she been offered a debrief-the-debriefers session following her intervention session, she might have been able to deal with her feelings immediately in a warm and supportive atmosphere and escaped the longer-term effects of vicarious traumatization.

Many of us who work in crisis intervention like to think that we are strong and brave and immune to the stress of working crisis situations. Strong and brave we might be, but vicarious traumatization is a real possibility in the field. Realistic expectations about our possible vulnerabilities can help us head off the dangers of working in crisis.

References

Bartemeier, L.H., Kubie, L.S., & Menninger, K. (1946). Combat exhaustion. *Journal of Nervous and Mental Disease, 146*, 359-389.

Diagnostic and Statistical Manual of Mental Disorders, Fourth Edition. (1994). Washington, D.C.: American Psychiatric Association, 424-427.

Figley, C.R. (1995). *Compassion Fatigue.* Levittown, PA: Brunner/Mazel Psychosocial Stress Series.

Herman, J. (1997). *Trauma and Recovery.* New York: Basic Books, Perseus Books Group.

Hudnall-Stamm, B. (2001). *Work-Related Secondary Traumatic Stress,* National Center for PTSD and White River Junction VAM & ROC, Dartmouth Medical School, Vermont. Article retrieved November 5, 2001, from www.ncptsd.org/research/rq/rqhtml/V8N2.html.

Kardiner, A., & Spiegel, H. (1947). *War, Stress and Neurotic Illness.* (rev. ed., The Traumatic Neurosis of War) New York: Hoeber, 1947), 1, cited in The Traumatic Neuroses of War: A Forgotten History, *Trauma and Recovery* (1997) J. Herman, New York: Basic Books, Perseus Books Group.

Krystal, H. (Ed.) (1968). *Massive psychic trauma.* New York: International Universities Press.

Lewinski, W. (1985-2000). Calibre Press, Street Survival Seminar (unpublished), 4101 International Parkway, Carrollton, TX 75007.

Marmar, C.R., Weis, D.S., Metzler, T.J., & Delucci, K.L. (1996). Characteristics of emergency services personnel related to peritraumatic dissociation during critical incident exposure. *American Journal of Psychiatry, 153* (7), 94-102.

Maslach, C., & Jackson, S.E. (1981). The measurement of experienced burnout. *Journal of Occupational Behavior, 2* (2), 99-113.

McCann, I.L., & Pearlman, L.A. (1990a). *Psychological trauma and the adult survivor: Theory, therapy and transformation.* New York: Brunner/Mazel.

McCann, I.L., & Pearlman, L.A. (1990b). Vicarious traumatization: A framework for understanding the psychological effects of working with victims. *Journal of Traumatic Stress, 3* (1), 131-149.

Pearlman, L.A., & MacIan, P.S., (1995). Vicarious Traumatization: An empirical study of the effects of trauma work on trauma therapists. *Professional Psychology: Research and Practice, 26,* 558-565.

Pearlman, L.A., & Saakvitne, K.W. (1995). *Trauma and the therapist: Countertransference and vicarious traumatization in psychotherapy with incest survivors.* New York: Norton.

Rainer, J.P. (1982). Compassion fatigue: When caregiving begins to hurt. In L. Vandercreek & T.L. Jackson (Eds.) Innovations In Clinical Practice: A sourcebook, Vol. 18 (pp. 441-453). Sarasota, FL: Professional Resource Press.

Valent, P. (1995). Survival strategies: A framework for understanding secondary traumatic stress and coping in helpers. In C.R. Figley (Ed.) *Compassion fatigue: Coping with secondary traumatic stress in those who treat the traumatized* (pp. 245 – 261). New York: Brunner/Mazel.

CHAPTER 4

The Effects of Trauma on Post-secondary Learning

By Kendall Johnson, Ph.D.

Overwhelming experiences profoundly affect our lives. They disrupt routine, interfere with life plans, and shake our expectations. Such critical events sometimes threaten our survival, present grotesque realities about the world, and bring permanent and unbearable loss.

The average high school student has experienced at least one such incident by age seventeen (Johnson, 1999), and by college graduation can be expected to have endured more. Reactions to these events can range from transient distress to extreme panic or shock. Post-crisis symptoms can be permanent and life changing. These symptoms can include a range from mild sleep or mood disturbances to serious depression, anxiety, or dissociative syndromes, or even result in full-blown Post-traumatic Stress Disorder.

Whether crisis occurs prior to or during collegiate enrollment, on campus or off, college students can be affected where it hurts the academic experience the most—learning. Professors, Deans, and support personnel can benefit from understanding the underlying chemistry of survival, its effects upon the process of learning, and steps that can be taken to assist student recovery from the crisis experience.

Chemistry of Survival

To understand the diverse and pernicious effects of trauma upon learning, a rudimentary and much simplified discussion of the neurochemical response to crisis is necessary and helpful. Everly (1989) has described the fight or flight emergency response to threat as a flooding of the system with three basic groups of neurohormones that have great survival value: catecholamines, corticosteriods, and endogenous opioids. When in balance, the effects of each complement the others to allow the body to respond optimally to life-threatening situations.

Fight or Flight Activators

Presented with a threat, the body must leave its resting state and act quickly. A flooding of catecholamines insures this. Catecholamines (e.g., epinephrine and norepinephrine) are released from the locus coeruleus to excite the system, triggering increased sympathetic nervous system activity. This fight or flight response is adaptive in the face of physical danger, prompting immediate action where inactivity could spell disaster.

The bad news of catecholamine flooding is that, unchecked, it can lead to mindless overreactivity and panic. Behavior can escalate from adaptive arousal to inappropriate and nondirective agitation. This condition, once referred to as "hysterical" behavior, precludes adaptive functioning.

Modulators

In order to mitigate such spiraling arousal, a concomitant flooding of a second class of neurochemicals serve to moderate and control the extremes of arousal in reaction to the catecholamine release. The anterior pituitary releases Adrenocorticotropic Hormone (ACTH) which activates a cascade of reactions, eventually including the release of glucocorticoids and cortisol. These modulate the reaction to the catecholamines, and keep the fight or flight response in check. This is very good news, as it serves to keep the behavioral response to crisis manageable. The physiology of arousal can be directed toward action in behalf of survival.

An inadequate release of glucocorticoids results in the failure to regulate the effects of catecholamines. The result is one form of acute stress response, over-reactivity to the crisis event or to reminders or memories of the crisis event. Key behavioral indicators include disorganization, agitation, and the inability to focus or control emotionality.

Another neurohormone related to the crisis response is serotonin, which also seems to modulate arousal. A neurotransmitter, serotonin helps activate a behavioral inhibition system that moderates over-reactivity. Low levels are associated with an exaggerated startle response, oversensitivity, and irritability.

Endogenous Opioids

The third group of neurohormones to flood the system in response to crisis is a set of naturally produced opioids. These serve the survival needs of the body by providing several adaptive reactions. First, the release of endogenous opioid peptides creates a heightened threshold for pain. Second, these opioids result in dissociative reactions, and a blunting of emotional reactions. Third, in combination with catacholamine flooding, increased levels of endogenous opioids result in amnesia reactions. Fourth, the opioids create a feeling of euphoria. Together these anesthetic, dissociative, amnesic, and euphoric reactions allow the individual to deal with overwhelming experiences adaptively, without succumbing to pain or emotion.

Too much endogenous opioid results in dissociation and shock-like behavior in which the individual is under-reactive and cannot act in his or her behalf.

These three sets of biochemicals flood the human system in the face of actual threat allowing adaptive survival behavior. However, this can also happen in nonthreatening circumstances such as lecture halls and study carrels. Adaptation to trauma requires ongoing psychological processing. As Horowitz (1986) has described, the psychological processing necessary to allow a trauma victim to successfully adapt his or her worldview requires satisfactory integration of the divergent experience. Both internal processing and external experiences can be interpreted by the primitive brain as threatening stimuli. Thus post-trauma processing can create internal cues, and reminders in the world can create external cues, both of which are interpreted as real threat. The brain is triggered into the emergency release of catecholamines, cortisoids, and opioids. This can happen at any time, including in the classroom.

Behavioral over- and under-reactivity may be signs of delayed activation of the survival chemical reactions due to delayed processing of the crisis experience. These reactions to internal chemical flooding can affect learning directly both in class and out, and can affect learning indirectly through developmental repercussions.

The Neuroanatomy of Failure

The effects of the flooding of neurohormones during crisis can include changes in the structure and function of the central nervous system. These changes can profoundly affect a student's ability to benefit from learning experiences. Several such changes have been verified by Bessel Van der Kolk (1996) through neuroimaging studies.

Van der Kolk cites a recently growing body of research that is beginning to outline the psychophysiology of trauma. The developmental effects of these neurohormonal responses appear to include disruption of the functional areas of numerous cortical and subcortical areas, including loss of synchronization and integration. Left hemisphere activities seem to be more affected, impacting language and recall abilities in particular. While the evidence is limited so far, it seems to provide support for observations leading to the new Complex Posttraumatic Stress Disorder discussed later in this chapter, which has particular relevance for children traumatized early and for prolonged periods. The potential for connections with a wide range of, thus far, poorly understood learning and adjustment problems among college people seems to be great.

Finally, as indicated above, researchers have narrowed the search for the brain centers responsible for these posttraumatic biological changes. Van der Kolk's neuroimaging has been especially helpful in this regard. According to him, two structures in the Limbic system (that part of the subcortical brain which is responsible for self preservation and survival) are critically affected by the chemistry released by the traumatic event. The first, the Amygdala, evaluates the emotional meaning of incoming stimulus, and integrates the representation of external events with emotional experiences associated with their memory. The second structure, the Hippocampus, categorizes, relates, and stores incoming stimuli in implicit, short term memory, a vital part of the process of creating and processing long-term, declarative memory.

Van der Kolk (1996) reports linking post-trauma chemical activity as described above with shrinking of the Hippocampus (due to sustained high levels of cortisol—a hormone toxic to the Hippocampus) and increased activity in the right hemisphere, site of parts of the Limbic system connected with the Amygdala. This would correlate with findings that activity in these various areas correspond with post-trauma symptoms.

The general roles of left and right hemispheres in learning are controversial. While popular literature holds the left hemisphere to be more of a "serial processor" (linear, sequential, analytic) while the right is more of a "parallel processor" (imagic, spatial, metaphoric), neuroscientists and educators find such generalities equivocal (Bruer, 1999). Despite this, Van der Kolk (1996) has found an interesting post-trauma phenomena: the Broca's Area in the left hemisphere is negatively affected by trauma, showing decreased blood flow and functioning. This correlates with the recognized symptom of "speechless terror" described by Terr (1990). The Broca's Area is associated with the process of transforming private experience into language, a part of the process of developing narrative memory.

Neurochemistry in the Lecture Hall

Following trauma the brain processes the traumatic material searching for survival clues for the future, and restructuring its worldview to take the traumatic experience into account. This integrative process is sometimes not differentiated from reality, and triggers an emergency chemical release when no danger is present. The resulting high levels of arousal directly affect brain functions critical to college success. These changes can result in difficulty in attending to lectures and presentations, reading, and cognitively processing curricular material (Ornitz & Pynoos, 1989; Pynoos, Steinberg, & Goenjian, 1996).

Attention and the Startle Reflex

One typical result of this is an inability to modulate the startle reflex. This means that any distraction not only causes a startle reflex, but any startle reflex spirals into a prolonged state of physiological arousal. Students who suffer from heightened startle reflex are victimized by the myriad of distractions that characterize a normal classroom. Further, any external cues—intended or unintended—in lecture or reading that is associated in the student's mind with the traumatic event may serve to trigger the startle reflex. Not only do startle reflexes break concentration and attention, but the subsequent internal chemical reaction makes attending to curricular material more difficult.

Dissociative Reactions

Dissociative reactions remove the student from the here and now, blunting consciousness and affect. They can be both short-term and long-term effects of endogenous opioid flooding. Dissociation is considered a key sign of trauma, both at the time of the incident and during the recovery period. Not only do dissociative reactions impact information access and retention; they also affect motivation and socialization. Attention and retention suffer when the student shuts down to the world.

Preoccupation

In the process of integrating trauma, memories and intrusive imagery often preclude focus upon schoolwork. When experiences do not fit existing models, the models must be revised and experiences reinterpreted until a "fit" is made. The predisposition to actively store and continually rework memories of incompletely "processed" experience, Horowitz (1986) calls a "completion tendency." To the extent the student is engaged in the attempt to process the memories and newly experienced realities presented by the traumatic experience, he or she is too preoccupied to fully benefit from the educational experience.

Concentration

External or internal cued flooding of the system with catecholamines increases sympathetic nervous activity and heightens physiological arousal, reducing the student's ability to concentrate. Similarly, decreased production of corticosteriods and serotonin result in inability to moderate the catecholamine-triggered fight or flight response. Normal curbs to the arousal level no longer work, and the arousal levels escalate. Impulses — such as aggression or emotionality — cannot be modulated, and they overcome cognitive controls.

Memory

Students who cannot classify, store, and retrieve information are at an obvious disadvantage in many classroom situations. Increased levels of endogenous opioids, triggered by the flooding of catecholamines, have detrimental effects upon memory retention and retrieval. Most college courses rely upon memory function. The ability to transfer and generalize learning, retrieve information in testing situations, and relate previously learned information to newly presented information is essential to university study.

Together these trauma-specific symptoms add up to significant obstacles to effective post-secondary learning. Unfortunately, that is not the end of it. Secondary effects can include the development of serious developmental and behavioral problems that are equally detrimental to the college experience.

Behavioral Development: On and Off Campus

The effects of trauma upon learning go beyond specific post-trauma symptoms, affecting in-class and out-of-class academic learning. Critical to college success is the management of normal developmental transitions. Learning requires more than books and lectures. It requires motivation, sustained effort, and commitment. If preoccupation with developmental issues and anxiety preoccupy the attention and energy of the student, academic learning suffers and the likelihood increases of behavioral difficulties inimical to college life.

Hardware and Conduct

As outlined above, changes in brain structure and function have been noted in persons suffering from traumatic stress (Van der Kolk, 1996). These changes can affect the integrated brain functioning necessary for higher academic learning. Students have difficulty moderating reactions to external and internal cueing, and develop behavior patterns intended to cope with the post-trauma symptoms. This behavior is likely to pose a significant distraction to others, and is frequently inappropriate to campus life. Campus security or local police may become involved, and instructors may refer such "troublesome" students for discipline. The student is at risk of becoming labeled and being treated as a troublemaker.

Typical Post-trauma Behavior

Three behavioral patterns associated with post-trauma response are behavioral regression, repetition compulsion, and risk taking. When faced with overwhelming stress, people tend to react to trauma by regressing to an earlier level of coping and readopt interests and behaviors associated with that level. In addition, one very natural way traumatic experiences can become integrated is through reenactment. The incident is repeatedly replayed literally or figuratively in an attempt to resolve the issues it has raised. Both regression and reenactments, however, put off others and lead to social rejection and additional labeling.

Normal and Not-so-normal Developmental Crises

Adults go through predictable growth stages as do children. Whether they are eighteen and newly enrolled, or returning to school for a mid-career shift, college students are subject to normal developmental crises where they must reorganize previous cognitive frameworks, emotional reaction patterns, coping strategies and spiritual dispositions to adapt to changing social and maturational demands (Erickson, 1967). These normal crises of development both affect and are affected by incidents that generate traumatic stress. Not only do developmental crises create specific vulnerabilities to traumas (e.g., identity formation, ego integrity, loss, etc.) but the recovery process from traumatic symptoms also complicates resolution of normal developmental crises. Thus developmental crises can exacerbate and be exacerbated by trauma.

In an interesting study of Vietnam veterans conducted in two phases, Wilson (1978) found symptom patterns reflecting Erickson's developmental issue approach. In the first part of that study, veterans struggled with issues related to Erickson's task of identity vs.

role confusion. The veterans' average age was then 25 (20 at time of combat service), and beyond the typical PTSD symptom configuration discussed above, the veterans were having particular difficulty in the area of adjustment to the existent social system of values and the maintenance of a sense of selfsameness and continuity. In the second phase of the study, the veteran's average age was 30. Beyond the expected range of more typical PTSD symptoms, the veterans at this stage were particularly challenged by life tasks having to do with resolving Erickson's task of intimacy vs. isolation. Veterans were having difficulty with issues of love relationships, personal friendships, responsibility toward jobs, and other commitments demanding propriety, reliability, and trustworthiness.

Thus traumas incurred prior to or during college can create symptoms that directly interfere with the learning process, creating a toxic interactive effect between symptoms and normal developmental crises. This package can make the stressors of post-secondary learning overwhelming, and reactions can take differing forms according to the student's age and developmental level.

Premature Structuring

Elkind (1981) studied children who, for various reasons, were thrust into the adult world prematurely. In following their performance and their life decisions, he determined that they had an unfortunate tendency to forego the normal process of gradual maturation and leap into binding decisions regarding their lives. At an earlier age than was necessary, they made career, marital, and schooling decisions that they lacked the experience to make. Based upon limited life experience, they "settled" for constricting life roles, personalities, and directions too quickly and without the benefit of normal post-adolescent exploration of themselves and the world. Elkind uses the term "premature structuring" to describe this propensity to define the self without the basis for more expansive and adaptive definition. Posttraumatic suffering can create a distrust of self and the world that tempts its victims to take "safe" courses and avoid the anxiety and uncertainty of delayed gratification.

Post-secondary learning is a commitment to delayed gratification. It demands sacrifice of life now to enhance life later, even when the benefits are uncertain. If the learner loses sight of the goal, and because of the trauma loses belief in the predictability of the future and the likelihood of the usefulness of the generic skills of post-secondary learning, he or she is likely to opt for more immediate results.

Turning In, Tuning Out, Dropping Out

Trauma can create serious biochemical and neuroanatomical difficulties in learning. Further, trauma can result in interruption and short-circuiting of the more subtle process of development. As a result, students can lose their competitive edge, become distracted and preoccupied with personal issues, and give up on their education. No study has ever documented the proportion of college dropouts whose dropping out was connected with traumatic events, but given the prevalence of trauma it is safe to assume that it is a substantial number.

Whatever that number, one fact remains. The majority of traumatic symptoms are transient, many are treatable with psychotherapeutic and pharmacological strategies with proven positive outcome, and much of the isolation and confusion of dealing with posttraumatic reactions can be mitigated with support.

Post-secondary institutions can intervene effectively with traumatized students, and by so doing, mitigate both short and long term difficulties with learning.

Assisting Traumatized Students

As indicated above, most post-crisis symptoms are transient, and the rate of spontaneous recovery is high. Trauma is a "done deal" term; the word trauma signifies lasting distress, and the distress generated by most negative life experiences is not lasting. Knowing this, then, the question becomes more specific: how can we help students avoid a lasting impact of situational crises upon their study?

Crisis Support

A key element in mitigating the effects of the crisis response is immediate care following the crisis. This volume will discuss the concept of Critical Incident Stress Management (Everly & Mitchell, 1999) and its application to school settings (Johnson, 1998, 2000; Johnson, Casey, Ertl, Everly, & Mitchell, 1999). The weaving together of individual and group crisis interventions, assessment, family support, organizational consultation, follow-up and referral following crisis events allows affected individuals, and the organization surrounding those individuals, comprehensive support. Toward this end crisis response teams trained in these interventions and familiar with the campus culture can be organized and made available.

Psychological Support

Brief psychotherapeutic interventions aimed at symptom management and adjustment may be effective and helpful. Some specific cognitive oriented therapies such as Cognitive Behavioral Therapy (Foa, Steketee, & Rothbaum, 1989) and body-oriented therapies such as Eye Movement Desensitization and Reprocessing (Shapiro, 1995), have been shown to provide effective relief from posttraumatic symptoms (Van der Kolk, 1996; Carbonell, & Figley, 1999). While efficacy studies show these short term psychotherapeutic approaches to be very promising, recommendation and referral to psychological intervention should take into account the student's readiness and willingness to access clinical assistance.

Medical Support

Students suffering from traumatic stress should be assessed for the possibility of medical support. Evaluation of neurological and physical symptoms should be considered, as well as prescription and monitoring of psychotropic medication when appropriate. Recent studies have been reported by Davidson and Van der Kolk (1996) to indicate several promising areas of pharmacological treatment. They point to dysregulation of the catecholaminergic system being amenable to treatment with MAO inhibitors, tricyclic antidepressives, as well as clonadine, benzo-diazapines, and beta-andregenic blockers. Davidson and van der Kolk discuss more recent data pointing to Fluoxetine and other selective seratonin uptake inhibitors (e.g., Prozac) being useful in managing PTSD symptoms, such as numbing and arousal, as well as depression. Post-trauma "kindling" effects, where lowered activation thresholds produce overarousal responses to the slightest stimuli, seem to be responsive to carbamazepine. Finally, they indicate anxiolytic drugs, such as clonazepam and buspirone, can be helpful with increased startle responsiveness. In any case, the purpose of psychotropic medication remains focused upon symptom relief, so those clients are able to participate more effectively in programs of learning and therapy. Medical doctors or psychiatrists at campus health centers can supervise medical intervention.

Social Intervention

Peer support is foundational to recovery from trauma (Ursano, Grieger, & McCarroll, 1996). Deliberate orchestration of social support can be used to combat social isolation and address symptoms as a community situation. Various support groups are often available on campus; some focused upon issues related to trauma, some on issues compounding the recovery process such as addiction, grief, or adjustment. In addition, informal support networks can be mobilized where appropriate through the offices of the dean of students, psychological services, or campus chaplain. Alternatively, existing peer networks can be augmented through education in recovery. Confidentiality is important, however, and must be maintained.

Learning Assistance

Colleges are becoming more adept in the provision of assistance for students who struggle with learning problems such as ADHD, dyslexia, visual or auditory impairments, and physical limitations. Such services can be utilized on a temporary basis for students suffering from posttraumatic complications that impair learning. The greatest assistance provided by such strategies as tutoring or adaptive techniques is often interpersonal. An incapacitating sense of isolation frequently follows traumatic events, as victims struggle with daunting workloads complicated by learning impairment. This is often offset by the additional attention provided by learning assistance.

Coaching

Exploring learning strategies, organization of work, and time management is often facilitated best by coaching. While tutorial assistance in specific subjects may be helpful, coaching focuses upon general approaches to all subjects and the maintenance of self-discipline, motivation, and personal performance. Coaches are often more readily accepted than counselors. As opposed to therapy or even group support, the coaching model is already congruent with many students' performance-based self image. Post-trauma learning frequently suffers from difficulties in concentration, memory, self-control, and behavior; coaching may assist in self-management and strategic planning.

While the effects of trauma on learning can be formidable and incapacitating, a well-orchestrated set of intervention and support services can be mobilized to assist students in maintaining their course of study and minimizing the disruption to their academic careers.

Some Speculation

We are learning a great deal about the effects of trauma upon learning on the biological and performance levels, and we are developing grounds upon which to predict its effect behaviorally and developmentally. At the same time, we are discovering measurably effective ways to intervene in the short and long-term aftermath of trauma to minimize its effect upon learning in academic contexts. A great deal, of course, remains a mystery. One area inviting speculation involves the future, particularly the effects of social change upon the outcome of trauma.

In this area there is reason for concern. Traditionally, the community has provided the supportive grounding for its traumatized members, and one of the most important predictors of recovery has been the context of the helping community. Yet this is a time of unparalleled social change, and the nature of community seems challenged by events.

At the turn of the last century Emile Durkheim (Jones, 1986) put forth a theory of suicide in which he posited social, not individual psychological, causes. Suicide rates are directly correlated with industrialization, he pointed out, and he theorized that suicide was the result of the internalization of the incompatible social forces of specialization. Reflecting the conflict of pre- and post-industrialist social values, the individual loses a cohesive value system or collective conscience. Anomie is the individual response to the breakdown of social norms, which in turn breaks down the individual's basis for knowing what to expect from others. Changing conditions lead to dissatisfaction, conflict, and deviance. Periods of social disruption lead to greater anomie. Some forms of deviation represent normal responses to frustrations, tensions, and stresses generated by conflicts in the structure of society.

What would Durkheim have made of society at the turn of this century? Would he see greater forces of contradiction, normlessness, and uncertainty? Might he be tempted to conclude that the individual is even less important now than a hundred years ago? The proper role of the individual seems to have changed from worker to consumer; we no longer generate goods and services so much as broker the flow of cash. We are valued, or perhaps pandered to, only to spend our money in this direction or that. Commercialism has replaced regionalism or nationalism, and local cultures are bought up. We are losing (or have sold) our sense of place. Identity—the task of adolescence and post-adolescence—is becoming a function of product loyalty, and values are replaced by price. Character is becoming a commodity. The traditional role of the post-secondary campus is changing along with the greater society, as is the purpose of higher education. The development of strong autonomy and character is becoming less important than commercial position.

These factors place the traumatized student at greater risk of failure in the university than ever before. As has been discussed, however, the university can take proactive steps to assist students in recovering from trauma and resuming productive study.

Like most else, the role of post-secondary education is undergoing transition. It remains to be seen how much the university will grow to reflect the current slide toward anonymous commercialism. Part of the acid test will be the manner in which it treats its wounded.

References

Bruer, J. (1999). "In search of...Brain-based education." Phi Delta Kappan. *79*, 648.

Carbonell, J., & Figley, C. (1999). "A systematic clinical demonstration of promising PTSD treatment approaches." *Traumatology. 1.*

Davidson, J., & Van der Kolk, B. (1996). "The psychopharmacological treatment of posttraumatic stress disorder." In B. Van der Kolk, A. McFarlane, and L. Weisaeth, (Eds.), *Traumatic Stress: The Effects of Overwhelming Experience on Mind, Body, and Society.* New York: Guilford.

Elkind, D. (2001). *The Hurried Child: Growing up too fast, too soon.* Cambridge, MA: Persens Books.

Erikson, E. (1967). *Identity, Youth and Crisis.* New York: Norton.

Everly, G. (1989). *A Clinical Guide to the Treatment of the Human Stress Disorder.* New York: Plenum Press.

Everly, G., & Mitchell, J. (1999). *Critical Incident Stress Management.* Ellicott City, MD: Chevron Publishing Company.

Figley, C. (1995). *Compassion Fatigue: Coping With Secondary Traumatic Stress Disorder in Those Who Treat the Traumatized.* New York: Brunner/Mazel.

Foa, E., Steketee, G., & Rothbaum, B. (1989). "Behavioral/cognitive conceptualizations of posttraumatic stress disorder." *Behavior Therapy, 20,* 155-176.

Horowitz, M. (1986). *Stress Response Syndromes.* New York: Jason Aronson.

Johnson, K. (1998). *Trauma in the Lives of Children: Crisis and Stress Management Techniques for Counselors, Teachers, and Other Professionals.* Alameda, CA: Hunter House Publishers.

Johnson, K. (2000). *School Crisis Management: A Hands-On Guide to Training Crisis Teams.* Alameda, CA: Hunter House Publishers.

Johnson, K., Casey, D., Ertl, B., Everly, G., & Mitchell, J. (1999). *School Crisis Response: A CISM Perspective.* Ellicott City, MD: Chevron Publishing Company.

Jones, R. (1986). *Emile Durkheim: An Introduction to Four Major Works.* Beverly Hills, CA: Sage Publications.

Ornitz, E., & Pynoos, R. (1989). "Startle modulation in children with posttraumatic stress disorder." *American Journal of Psychiatry, 147,* 866-870.

Pynoos, R., Steinberg, A., & Goenjian, A. (1996). "Traumatic stress in childhood and adolescence: Recent developments and current controversies." In B. van der Kolk, A. McFarlane, and L. Weisaeth. 1996. *Traumatic Stress: The Effects of Overwhelming Experience on Mind, Body, and Society.* New York: Guilford Press.

Shapiro, F. (1995). *Eye Movement Desensitization and Reprocessing.* New York: Guilford Press.

Terr, L. (1990). *Too Scared To Cry: Psychic Trauma In Childhood.* New York: Basic Books.

Ursano, R., Grieger, T., & McCarroll, J. (1966). "Prevention of Posttraumatic Stress: Consultation, Training, and Early Treatment." In Van der Kolk, B., A. McFarlane, and L. Weisaeth. *Traumatic Stress: The Effects of Overwhelming Experience on Mind, Body, and Society.* New York: Guilford Press.

Van der Kolk, B., McFarlane, A., & Weisaeth, L. (1996). *Traumatic Stress: The Effects of Overwhelming Experience on Mind, Body, and Society.* New York: Guilford Press.

Wilson, J. (1978). *Identity, Ideology and Crisis: The Vietnam Veteran in Transition.* 2 vols. Washington, D.C.: Disabled American Veterans.

CHAPTER 5

Working with Parents of College and University Students

By Russell Lee, Ed.D.

Following a traumatic event on a college campus, college officials may need to respond to the parents of students as well as to the university community itself. Parents may call with concerns about the safety and well-being of their children, and may wish information about the event. Parents who are distant from the campus may be particularly upset, quite understandably, because of a lack of reassurance that might come if they could physically hold and comfort their child. Even parents close to the scene may be frustrated because college students, often at an age of increasing independence, may resist parental comfort and see parental intervention as interference.

An additional difficulty is that while some of the information requested by parents is public ("Yes, a tornado struck the campus at 1 p.m. Two campus buildings were seriously damaged, but no one was injured. Students are still being housed in the residence halls, which remain undamaged"), other information may be private, given the adult legal status of the students. The Family Educational Rights and Privacy Act limits the information that colleges can release about students.

Limitations on the Release of Information

The Family Educational Rights and Privacy Act (FERPA) (20 U.S.C. § 1232g; 34 CFR Part 99) is a Federal law that protects the privacy of student education records. The law applies to all schools that receive funds under an applicable program of the U.S. Department of Education.

FERPA gives parents certain rights with respect to their children's education records, but these rights transfer to the student in large part when he or she reaches the age of 18 or attends a school beyond the high school level. Generally, colleges and universities must have written permission from a matriculated student in order to release any information from the student's education record. However, FERPA allows schools to disclose those records, without consent, to the following parties or under the following conditions (34 CFR § 99.31):

- School officials with legitimate educational interest;
- Other schools to which a student is transferring;
- Specified officials for audit or evaluation purposes;
- Appropriate parties in connection with financial aid to a student;
- Organizations conducting certain studies for or on behalf of the school;
- Accrediting organizations;
- To comply with a judicial order or lawfully issued subpoena;
- Appropriate officials in cases of health and safety emergencies; and
- State and local authorities, within a juvenile justice system, pursuant to specific state law.

Note that parents are not among the listed parties. Schools may disclose to parents or to anyone, without consent, "directory" information such as a student's name, address, telephone number, date and place of birth, honors and awards, and dates of attendance, but this information is, of course, not what parents want to hear following a campus crisis.

The Family Educational Rights and Privacy Act gives college students themselves certain rights with respect to their education records. These rights are:

- The right to look at their own educational records within 45 days of the day the university receives a request for access.
- The right to request the amendment of their own education record if that they believe it is inaccurate or misleading.
- The right to consent to disclosures of personally identifiable information contained in their education records, except to the extent that FERPA authorizes disclosure without consent. One exception,

which permits disclosure without consent, is disclosure to school officials with legitimate educational interests. A school official has a legitimate educational interest if the official needs to review an education record in order to fulfill his or her professional responsibility. Another exception is to Law Enforcement.

- The right to file a complaint with the U.S. Department of Education concerning alleged failures by the University to comply with the requirements of FERPA.

Thus, the Family Educational Rights and Privacy Act allows for information about students to be communicated within the institution and to outside agencies such as Law Enforcement, but does not allow for information from written records to be given to parents without prior written consent by the student.

According to Ingrid Brault (personal communication), Program Specialist with the Family Policy Compliance Office, FERPA generally requires that an educational agency or institution obtain written consent before disclosing education records or personally identifiable information from education records (34 CFR 99.30 and 99.31). FERPA defines "education records" as: those records, files, documents, and other materials, which (i) contain information directly related to a student; and (ii) are maintained by an educational agency or institution or by a person acting for such agency or institution (20 U.S.C. 1232g(a)(4)(A); 34 CFR 99.3). Although FERPA generally prohibits the nonconsensual disclosure of information derived from education records, there are certain exceptions to this general prohibition. 20 U.S.C. § 1232g(b); 34 CFR § 99.30 and 99.31. One of these exceptions permits the nonconsensual disclosure of information derived from education records to that student's parent if the student is a dependent student, as defined in section 152 of the Internal Revenue Code of 1986. 20 U.S. C. § 1232g(b)(1)(H); 34 CFR § 99.31(a)(8), essentially meaning that the parents claim the student on their federal income tax. Further, neither the age of the student nor the parent's status as custodial parent is relevant to determining whether disclosure of information from the education records of eligible students to a parent without written consent is permissible under FERPA. If a student is claimed as a dependent by either parent for tax purposes, then either parent may have access under this provision.

It is also important to point out that FERPA applies to the disclosure of *tangible* records and of information derived from tangible records. FERPA does not protect the confidentiality of information in general, and, therefore, does not apply to the disclosure of information derived from a source other than education records, even if education records exist which contain that information. As a general rule, information that is obtained through personal knowledge or observation, and not from an education record, is not protected from disclosure under FERPA. Cf. Kline v. Department of Health & Human Services, 927 F.2d 522 (10th Cir. 1991)(Privacy Act); Thomas v. Department of Energy, 719 F.2d 342 (10th Cir. 1983)(Privacy Act); Savarese v. Harris, 620 F.2d 298 (5th Cir. 1980) (Privacy Act), cert. denied, 449 U.S. 1078 (1982).

So in an emergency, the Family Educational Rights and Privacy Act can be stretched a bit, in that it only applies to written records, and even then, if the student is a dependent, his or her parents can still have access to information. In an emergency, however, you may not have easy access to information regarding whether or not the student is a dependent.

If a dependent student is killed or seriously injured, his or her parents *can* be called with the information. In an emergency, when parents call to find out how their children are doing, school officials can go beyond giving out directory information about a student, and volunteer to go find the student to see if they are OK. Exceptions are also made in the case of drug or alcohol abuse. Colleges get broad latitude to reveal the results of disciplinary proceedings against students accused of violent crimes, and to notify parents if a student younger than 21 is caught drinking or using illegal drugs. In general, however, only the most basic written information can be released if the student is not a dependent. Information such as whether the student has been attending classes or whether they have been to the counseling center because they are depressed, if acquired from written records, cannot be released. When a parent is concerned, sometimes the only thing a school official can do is to agree to find the students and encourage them to call their parents. Personal observations can be communicated to the parents unless the student has been promised confidentiality, such as by counseling center staff.

One additional bit of good news is that colleges and universities may be protected from lawsuit by individuals. The U.S. Supreme Court ruled 7-2 recently on Gonzaga v. Doe, that FERPA may not be enforced via private lawsuits. The ruling established that students or parents may not go to the court to enforce FERPA. Writing for the majority, Chief Justice William H. Rehnquist said that for a federal law to be enforceable through a private lawsuit, it must be clear that the plaintiff was "within the general zone of interest that the statute is intended to protect," and that Congress clearly intended to authorize individuals to go to court. He said that FERPA was not such a law.

The case, number 01-679, was an appeal by a university in Spokane, Washington, following a judgment of more than $1 million to a former education student who was denied a state teaching license after a professor had included an otherwise unsubstantiated accusation of sexual misconduct in the student's record. The Court's decision means that individuals cannot sue colleges and universities for damages under FERPA. The ruling does not mean that educational institutions can share personal information on students, however.

You can find information on the U.S. Supreme Court decision at http://a257.g.akamaitech.net/7/257/2422/20jun20021230/www.supremecourtus.gov/opinions/01pdf/01-679.pdf

The name and address of the office that administers the Family Educational Rights and Privacy Act is:

Family Policy Compliance Office
U.S. Department of Education
400 Maryland Avenue, S.W.
Washington, DC 20202-4605

For additional information or technical assistance, you may call (202) 260-3887 (telephone), or (202) 260-9001 (fax). Individuals who use TDD may call the Federal Information Relay Service at 1-800-877-8339.

Given these limitations on the release of information, can college and university officials still do an effective job of working with parents? Yes, with some restrictions (see Table 5-1).

Working with Individual Parents

Individual parents may call you on the phone, requesting information about the campus crisis and about how their child is doing. They are very likely to be upset and not acting at peak capacity. Your communication skills, and in particular your listening skills, become very important.

When talking with parents, it is important to pay attention to both the parent's verbal and nonverbal messages. The cognitive content of a message is usually fairly easy to identify, but when the speaker is upset, as parents may be under these circumstances, their verbal messages can be vague and incomplete. We need to draw the speaker out to encourage them to present their full message, and we need to get feedback on

Table 5-1
Responses To Parents' Questions

Questions Parents May Ask	Possible Responses
What plans are in place to make sure that this tragedy does not happen again?	Tell them what plans are in place. Reassure them about your concern for the safety of the students. Listen to their underlying concerns and respond empathetically.
What sort of crisis responses should I look for in my son?	Inform them of possible crisis responses while normalizing the fact that symptoms do often occur. Listen for what their concerns are.
What strategies can you suggest for me to help my daughter cope with this experience?	Discuss such strategies. Help them tailor the strategies to their own situation as they see their relationship to their daughter.
I'd like to know if my son has been keeping up his class attendance since the tragedy.	I can see that you are worried about your son. I will contact him and discuss his class attendance with him and ask how he is doing.
How have my daughter's test grades been since the incident?	Her test grades are confidential. Can you talk with her about this? Let's discuss some ways you might approach her.
I am worried about my son's drinking in the last month since the incident. Has he gotten into trouble because of it?	If he has gotten into trouble because of drinking, this information can be revealed, and possibly the parents' help enlisted. If he has not gotten into trouble, you can still empathize with their concerns and tell them what resources are available.
I am worried about my daughter.	Draw the parents out using listening skills. Come up with a plan of action for them to use.

our understanding in order to determine whether we have heard the message correctly. The nonverbal aspects of their messages are also important. Feelings are often carried in vocal tone, pitch, vocal inflections, and other nuances of nonverbal communication, and feelings are usually a crucial aspect of the parent's message. Contradictions between verbal and nonverbal messages require special notice and care. When the parent says "I'm not really concerned; I just thought I'd call" in a somewhat shaky and apprehensive tone we need to take the nonverbal message of worry seriously even though it is dismissed by the verbal message.

Barriers to Listening

Many things can come between you and your ability to listen thoroughly to the parent's message. Among them are making value judgments and having selective (or just plain wrong) perceptions about the parent or the kind of person the parent is. It is best to withhold judgment about the parent, and instead to listen with full engagement. Some speakers pause between paragraphs of their speech. If we are too quick to respond, they may not feel listened to fully, or even at all! Three techniques are particularly useful in helping listen with full engagement: the skills of attending, supporting, and clarifying.

Attending Skills

Attending skills are those that allow you to listen as fully as possible to the parent, and that communicate to the parent that you are fully listening. The latter part of this definition is very important. Were you to listen closely to a speaker with your eyes closed, humming a song, and making incongruent facial expressions, even if you remembered perfectly what the speaker said, the speaker would assume that you did not hear them correctly. Many people feel most listened to when the speaker engages in direct but not prolonged eye contact, nods from time to time, uses an attentive body posture, makes sounds of understanding, and displays congruent facial expressions. Nonverbal mechanisms such as these, however, vary from culture to culture. It is best to look at the speaker's nonverbal behavior to try to determine if they perceive you as listening well. It their eyes are downcast and they look uncomfortable, consider whether your eye contact is too prolonged.

When listening, we need to be trying to understand the essential message of the speaker, which may sometimes be a bit different than their actual words. This requires listening to the phrases they use, of course, but also paying attention to their feelings and their nonverbal language, in the light of what we know about their culture, background and experience.

There are three types of basic attending skills:

1. *Minimal encourages* are the short verbal equivalent of a head nod, such as "Mm-hmm," or "I see." Such interjections serve the function of telling the speaker that you are listening, but that you do not want to interrupt their flow of conversation.

2. *Paraphrasing* is saying back to the speaker, ideally in new words, the core of meaning of what they just said to you. It communicates to the speaker that you heard them accurately, if you did, and gives them a

chance to correct your impression if you did not. It also gives you an opportunity to focus or lead the speaker a bit, since you only paraphrase the most productive portion of what they say. A difficulty with paraphrasing is that it is hard to do well without seeming like you are using a psychological technique on the speaker. Skill at paraphrasing requires a lot of practice.

3. *Reflection of feeling* involves reflecting back to the speaker the emotions either explicit or implicit in their speech, as in "you must be feeling quite worried now." It often involves a bit of guesswork on the part of the listener, but if you guess accurately, it can produce real progress in helping the speaker feel understood..

Supporting Skills

Providing support builds a relationship foundation between you and the parent you are listening too. Good use of the attending skills mentioned above is very helpful towards this end, but there are specific supporting skills too. In order to show support we need to communicate an atmosphere of security, reassurance and encouragement, and communicate that we respect the parent's dignity and worth. Often this atmosphere is conveyed nonverbally, with appropriate eye contact, warm and understanding facial expressions, open body language, and vocal tones that are neither condescending nor dismissive, but rather are friendly and informal.

Interjections such as "I see," and "That must have been horrible for you," or even "Mm-hmm" if done properly can act as place holders during the parent's speech, letting them know that you are listening to them without interrupting their flow of speech, and giving you the opportunity to show that you are feeling supportive, understanding, and respectful. When a parent is worrying and in pain, consoling them is an excellent means of communicating support.

Clarifying Skills

Clarifying is not really done to increase your understanding of the issues (although that may happen when you clarify); your understanding is increased primarily through the attending skills discussed above. Clarifying skills are used to help make various issues clearer to the parent. If we feign understanding of something unclear that the parent has just said, that may keep the parent talking, but it fails to take into account the possibility that the thoughts behind what they just said were unclear to them too, or were only partially formed when they began to speak. The clarifying response encourages the parent to think about, restate, or even redefine a statement that they just made. Paired with good attending skills, the request for clarification may help the parent to refine the thoughts behind what they have just said, and to understand their own position better.

Clarifying responses, like all responses, need to be accompanied by congruent nonverbal expressions, in this case showing the parent that you are sincerely interested, but do not yet quite understand.

There are three types of clarifying skills:

1. *Perception checking* involves some guessing about what the parent means, and asking them if your perception is accurate. You might say "It sounds to me that your major worry is that your son is going to be too upset to be able to study, is that right?" if you think that that is a major worry that needs to be focused on, but it was jumbled in with many more minor concerns that the parent expressed, and that you are having some trouble sorting out. If you are correct that this is the major concern, both you and the parent can recognize it, and can then pursue it.

2. *Clarification of alternatives* can be used when you are less sure what the parent's major concerns are, and you need to know so that you can help focus your time together. You might say something like "We have talked about several things now, and I am not sure which is the most important for us to focus on. Which do you see as the more pressing issue, your concern about your daughter because of the loss of her roommate or your surprise at her sudden decision to change majors?" Of course you might end up talking about both, but it works well to begin with the one most upsetting to the parent.

3. *Requests for elaboration* involve requests for specific pieces of information. To the vague "I am afraid that my daughter will do something...unfortunate." You might respond, "Tell me what you mean by 'unfortunate,'" or you might say, "Do you mean that you think that she is considering suicide?"

All of these skills—attending skills, supporting skills and clarifying skills—are necessary to help a parent who comes to you with concerns after a campus crisis to feel thoroughly listened to, and helped to focus on what their main concerns are. At this point, the two of you should be able to come up with alternatives that will reduce their concerns and make headway towards potential solutions.

Working with Groups of Parents

Another post-crisis challenge may be working with groups of parents who come to the campus in order to pick up their children and bring them home, or else to confirm that the situation is stabilized and that the children are ok. When parents actually come to the campus and can see and hug their children post crisis, the parents can see for themselves how their children are doing. Their needs from you may be more for information and reassurance about how the crisis is being managed than information about their individual child.

One useful technique for working with parents to give them information about the details of the incident and how it is being managed, is the Crisis Management Briefing (CMB).

Crisis Management Briefings are a large group intervention technique, explained in much greater detail in Chapter Six on the core components of Critical Incident Stress Management. CMBs can consist of a series of small group meetings, or can be used with large groups of people if necessary, and the groups can combine parents and students. Among the basic goals of a CMB, are to:

1. Provide information
2. Provide rumor control
3. Reduce the sense of chaos that can appear following tragedy
4. Provide coping resources
5. Facilitate follow-up care
6. Improve cohesion and morale
7. Determine whether there are any other group needs

The Crisis Management Briefing is a four-step intervention model. The four steps are assembly, information, reactions, and strategies. These steps are explained in detail in Chapter 6.

How to Make a Referral

Sometimes in working with people who have been exposed to crisis situations or with the loved ones of people involved in a crisis, it is important to make a referral. Therapeutic intervention can be an important part of Critical Incident Stress Management (CISM). While many CISM techniques are both short term and designed to reduce the need for longer term intervention, an additional strength of these techniques is that they may make a referral for more long term intervention possible, by bringing people in crisis to the attention of crisis experts. It is difficult for some people to make a referral. We may be afraid that the person we are referring will feel that we are meddling in his or her personal affairs, or will be embarrassed, or will think that we think that they are crazy, or will feel that we are acting superior. It is important to remember that you are making a referral out of compassion and concern. Such feelings do not mean we think that we are superior; they mean that we care.

Know Appropriate Resources

The first step in making an effective referral is to know about appropriate resources. You should know the mental health providers in your community and region, and you should know the kind of clients with whom they work best. Referrals are most effective when you can name and give additional information about the professional to whom you are making the referral. "I think that you should see Mary Smith in the University Counseling Service. Mary has had a lot of experience in working with people who have been exposed to significant trauma, such as you have, and she seems to really understand what going through a crisis is like. Here is her telephone number."

You cannot personally know resources very widely outside your community and region, but you can still make a referral. Most communities have a community mental health center or satellite office to which you can refer. Many businesses have an EAP designated to provide initial consultation and follow-up referrals, and the person you are referring may know how to contact their EAP if they have one. The following web sites can be helpful:

American Psychiatric Association, www.psych.org
American Psychological Association, www.apa.org
MentalHealth.Com, www.mentalhealth.com/main.html
Mental Health Infosource, www.mhsource.com/
Mental Health Net, www.cmhc.com
National Alliance for the Mentally Ill (NAMI), www.namilorg/index.html
National Association of Social Workers, www.socialworkers.org

Make the Referral

I prefer to write down the name and number of the mental health professional to whom I am referring. Just writing a referral on a piece of paper is not enough, though. While it is usually best to let the person you are referring handle as many of the details as possible, they may question whether their problems really are severe enough to warrant seeing a professional; they may be afraid of broken confidentiality, cold and uncaring professionals, or whether they will be really understood and accepted. The person you are referring may not know the actual details of how to make an appointment. Discussing these details may put them at ease.

Following through dramatically increases the success of a referral. You can increase the client's willingness to accept the referral by naming and describing the mental health professional you are referring to, sometimes by letting them know that you are going to call the mental health professional in advance to brief them (reducing the concern of the person you are referring about telling their story), and even by dialing the phone for the client and standing by while they make the appointment. In rare instances you may need to accompany the them to an appointment.

Follow-up

Further contact after making a referral is not essential, but it does communicate to the people you have referred that you are interested in their well being, and not just trying to get rid of them to someone else. If they have not maintained their appointments, following up may help you discover that, so that you can make a more effective referral.

Following up also helps you evaluate. You can find out how well your referral strategies worked, and you can find out whether the mental health professional you referred to was a good match for this person. Both pieces of information are useful to you in helping you improve how you refer.

Summary

There are limits on the nature and amount of information that we can give to parents following a campus crisis. We may not be able to communicate to the parents the written educational records of their children. We can, however, listen with compassion and understanding, help focus the conversation on productive areas, pursue solutions to the parents' concerns, provide information on stress and stress recovery, and make referrals as appropriate.

Doing these things will reduce the negative effect of campus tragedies on the parents of the affected students, and may help them to help their children.

CHAPTER 6

Critical Incident Stress Management: The Core Components

By Dan Casey, Ed.D.

This chapter will address Critical Incident Stress Management (CISM) and the core elements of Critical Incident Stress Management. In depth demonstrations of the core components listed here are in Chapters 7 and 8 of this book.

Definition of Critical Incident Stress Management

CISM is the name given to a specific type or structure of crisis interventions or trauma response. This name was developed by the International Critical Incident Stress Foundation to identify a specific type of intervention and was developed by Jeffrey T. Mitchell. It was originally used in the field of emergency services, but has since been adapted to work in public safety applications, school settings, college and university settings, and business and industry settings, in addition to the emergency settings.

CISM is a comprehensive, integrated, multicomponent crisis intervention system (Everly and Mitchell, 1999; Flannery, 1999). CISM is a program that spans the complete crisis continuum (Everly & Mitchell, 1997). It is comprehensive in that it spans the three phases of the crisis: pre-crisis, acute crisis, and post-crisis. (Everly & Mitchell, 1997) In each of these phases, CISM provides a finite, structured intervention program to address those issues inherent in that specific phase. It is integrated in that it contains a number of interventions or components, each developed to fit a specific use or need. Each also integrates or interacts with the other. Others are used to lead from on-scene intervention to post-crisis interventions.

CISM is multidimensional in that it contains a number of components, each providing a specific function, dependent upon the incident and the reactions to the incident.

Depending upon the team needs and situations, the number and importance of the components will vary. For example, many colleges and universities have a crisis plan that addresses physical safety needs, but do not have a crisis response team developed that addresses the human factors portion of a traumatic event. Other colleges and universities have this in place, but have not developed a way to get that information out to those on campus that would access them if they were known about. Specific components of the CISM address each of these issues.

Core Components of CISM

There are many crisis intervention techniques. At a minimum, CISM consists of 10 core components. Five are specific interventions and five others are strategic applications or methods. According to the Operations Manual published by the International Critical Incident Stress Foundation (ICISF) (Mitchell & Everly, 2001), the interventions are:

- Demobilizations
- Crisis management briefings
- Defusings
- Debriefings
- Individual interventions

Variations of using these five interventions are addressed in:

- Family CISM
- Organizational consultations
- Pastoral crisis interventions

All interventions and uses are addressed prior to an incident with pre-crisis preparation, and all interventions include either follow-up or referral. These are the final two of the 10 core elements.

In addition to the 10 core components listed, there are a number of "other components" that may be utilized depending upon the situation and the needs of the entity being served. These include:

- Pre-incident traumatic stress education
- Continuing stress education

- Administrator and supervisor stress education and support programs
- Peer counseling
- Professional counseling
- On-scene support services
- Disaster intervention services
- Research and development
- Other support services as provided

CISM Definitions

The following is a brief introduction of terms to serve as a basis for consistency in understanding the CISM process.

Cumulative Stress—stress that erodes coping mechanisms

Crisis—the response to an event

Critical Incident—any event that has the potential to cause the crisis response (also see "Trauma")

Crisis Intervention—psychological "first aid"

Critical Incident Stress Management (CISM)—a comprehensive, integrated, multicomponent crisis intervention system consisting of a set of core components.

Posttraumatic Stress—very intense stress arousal following a traumatic stressor

Posttraumatic Stress Disorder—the official diagnosis (DSM-IV, 1994) of a posttraumatic stress syndrome with specific characteristics

Stress—the nonspecific response of the body to any demand placed on it

Stressor—the stimulus that causes, evokes, or is otherwise associated with stress

Stress Management—the conscious effort to better control, mitigate, or interact with the stress in one's life

Target Organs—that part of the mind or body that is the target of the stress response and develops signs and symptoms of overarousal

Trauma—any event outside the usual realm of experience that is distressing (see "Critical Incident")

CISM Group Interventions

The following information gives an in-depth description of the group interventions and identifies when each is typically used.

Demobilization

A demobilization (Mitchell & Everly, 2001) is a quick information and rest session that is provided when emergency services units, having responded to calls outside their usual response area, are released from service to return to their home duty station. It can also be used to identify those individuals that may need assistance when they return home. It is used only with emergency services workers. A demobilization consists of two parts: the first is a 10-minute informational session, the second is 20 minutes for food and rest. It is provided to teams of workers, i.e., fire departments, ambulance units, law enforcement teams, dog teams, and special units. It is provided by trained CISM team members, either peers or mental health professionals.

During the informational session, the workers are brought up to date on what has happened on the site since they arrived. They are told about some reactions they can expect to experience because of what they have just been through. They are also given some strategies on how to manage those reactions that they might have. If further interventions are planned or necessary, they are informed that this will occur. The leaders of this group are given a chance to share anything they need to share at this time.

The CISM team members providing this demobilization also assess the groups to see if anyone is showing excessive signs of stress. If such is the case, the affected person is talked to right there, or word is sent back to their home station that a local CISM team should be aware that they have persons affected by this event and may need to take appropriate action.

Following this short intervention, the group is taken to another room where the host group has provided high protein, low sugar, low cholesterol, and non-caffeinated products for their consumption. CISM team members may circulate from table to table, but no intervention is provided. The group is usually free to return to their home station following the rest and food break.

Most college and university teams will never get involved in a demobilization, but they should understand what a demobilization is and what it involves (Mitchell & Everly, 2001).

Crisis Management Briefings

Crisis Management Briefings (CMB) (Mitchell & Everly, 2001) are a large group intervention technique. They are designed to be used with large groups of victims (up to 300 persons). They are typically used following mass disasters or for students and parents following an event on the university property or on campus. They are also used very successfully with employees in the business world, as well as by military units for enlisted personnel and their families. The CMB can be applied following acts of terrorism, mass disasters, community violence, school crises, college and university crises, workplace violence, and military crises.

The basic goals of a CMB are: to provide information, to provide rumor control and reduce the sense of chaos, to provide coping resources, to facilitate follow-up care, to engender increased cohesion and morale, and to assess the further needs of the group and restore personnel to adaptive functions (Mitchell & Everly, 2001).

The CMB is a four-step intervention model that is easily adaptable to almost any given situation. The four steps are: assembly, information, reactions, and strategies.

Step One: Assembly

This step consists of bringing together a group of individuals who experienced a common crisis event. For example, in response to a crisis event that occurred on campus, planning for the CMB would include selecting a location (such as the campus theater) of sufficient size to accommodate the number of students, faculty, and staff that are affected. Depending upon the crisis event and the number of people affected, one dormitory or one class might be addressed at a time.

Planning for this step also includes identifying how the notices and information about the CMB will be shared with the intended audience. Is there a television station or local radio station that most of the group listen to? Are there newspapers to spread the word, etc.? Can flyers be posted around campus? What is the usual method of sharing information on the campus? This step serves as the first step in reestablishing a sense of community. This is very important to the recovery and building process following a crisis event.

Step Two: Information

This component is the greatest step provided for giving the persons in the CMB back some control in their lives. Sharing appropriate information from a reliable, credible source is invaluable. This information should be shared by the most appropriate and credible source available. For example, if the incident involved a fire, then the fire chief should give the information. If it is a law enforcement issue, then the highest ranking law enforcement person should give this information. If that individual is not available, the president of the university should share the information, or if he is not available, then a vice-president would step in. This assists in the perceived credibility of the message and assures the group that the actions taken will be effective.

The information being shared is the *facts* of the event. Objective and credible information serves to dispel *rumors* about the event, to reduce anticipatory anxiety, and to return a sense of control to the victims. The group should be told as much as is known (and not known) about the event.

Step Three: Reactions

This step is provided by credible mental health professionals. Using those mental health personnel most recognized on campus will engender trust that the information being shared is the best information available, shared by those that know the most about reactions to any given event. The presenters discuss the common reactions to this event that many persons will experience. They discuss the signs, symptoms, and themes that are relevant to the incident, i.e., in the case of suicide, the psychological themes of suicide would be addressed. Common signs and symptoms such as feelings of grief, anger, and guilt; loss of sleep and appetite; and other psychological and physiological reactions to an event should be shared.

Step Four: Strategies

This step is also provided by a mental health professional and addresses such things as self-care and personal coping strategies that are of value in mitigating the impact of such an event. Simple and practical stress management activities are talked of and shared. Community and campus resources that are available to the victims are identified and addressed in this step. Handouts with the most pertinent information should be available for group members to take with them. Questions may be entertained at this point, depending on the event and the group's reactions.

Many schools, colleges, and universities have found the need to add another step here. They break the large group into smaller groups (12 to 18) and meet in a small group format for 15 minutes. The small groups are led by CISM team members. The groups discuss what they are feeling and frustrated with, and come up with one or two recommendations for the leaders of this CMB. The entire group then meets again and each small group shares what they have come up with.

CMBs can be provided as often as necessary. For instance, in a recent event at a nearby college, one of the professors was jailed for molesting a student. CMB were provided to many classes, dorms, and groups on campus following the arrest, again following the trial, and again the next year when students returned to campus. CMBs are the easiest form of crisis intervention to provide, and they reach the largest number of individuals of any crisis event.

Defusings

Defusings (Mitchell & Everly, 2001) are small group interventions provided on the scene during the incident, or provided away from the scene immediately after an incident is over. A defusing can be provided at the end of a shift. For instance, if a crisis event happens early on the campus security's 8-hour shift, the campus CISM team could provide a defusing at the end of that shift. Defusings are provided to small groups of affected personnel. Many defusings may be provided for the same event, depending upon how many persons are affected and to what degree. Defusings should always be provided by trained CISM team members. Defusings are often provided by peers, i.e., others on campus who share the same type of environment.

The goals of a defusing are:

- To mitigate the impact of an event
- To accelerate the recovery process
- To assess the need for other CISM services
- To reduce physical, emotional, cognitive, behavioral, and spiritual symptoms of distress

The defusing process does the following:

- Establishes a nonthreatening environment
- Allows for rapid ventilation
- Equalizes the information
- Restores cognitive processing of the event
- Provides information for stress survival
- Affirms the value of the person involved
- Establishes linkages for additional support
- Develops expectancies for the future

The defusing has three phases or steps. These steps are: introduction, exploration, and information.

Introduction

This step is used to introduce the facilitator, identify the event, state the purpose of the CISM team, and motivate the participants to get involved in the process. Things shared in this step include:

- Putting the event into context
- Setting the rules of the defusing
- Stressing that confidentiality is the key to the defusing process
- Reassuring the participants that this is not a critique nor an investigation, nor is it psychotherapy
- Stating the goals of the defusing
- Describing the process of the defusing
- Providing/offering additional support

Exploration

This defusing step is designed so that the individuals involved can get a clearer picture of what actually happened. People are asked to describe what happened, clarifying questions are asked, and those persons involved in the incident share their experiences and reactions. The CISM team does not dig into their feelings, but does allow them to vent whatever emotions they wish. The team assesses the need for further interventions, and assures the group that they will provide help as needed to assist them in processing this event.

Information

This last step of the defusing process provides the group with information. The CISM team acknowledges and summarizes the information provided by the participants in the exploration step. They then share the following information:

- You are normal persons having normal reactions to an abnormal event
- Do not fight the reactions you are having
- Give your mind and body time to process this event
- Watch your diet and control stimulant consumption for the next few days
- Be aware help is available
- Seek support and help from each other
- Seek support and help from your significant others

- Return to and maintain the routine you had before the event as soon as possible

Follow-up services by the CISM team are always necessary after a defusing to assure that the personnel are managing their stress adequately. This assures that additional interventions are provide as needed.

Critical Incident Stress Debriefing

A Critical Incident Stress Debriefing (CISD) (Mitchell & Everly, 2001) is a 7-step or phase post-crisis group process that is used only after an event is over. It is not a "hurry up" intervention, and the debriefing should be held when the participants are emotionally "ready" to accept and benefit from a debriefing. This "psychological window" for using the CISD must be open in order for the debriefing to accomplish what it is meant to accomplish. Whereas the defusing was provided immediately following an event, the debriefing may be 2, 3, or even 5 days, after the event has ended. Demonstrations in the use of this specific crisis intervention are in Chapter 8 of this book.

The purpose of the CISD is to lead a group of persons from a cognitive perspective of the incident, back through the emotions experienced at the worst part of the incident, and then back again to a cognitive level, while lowering the stress reactions to the event and allowing those being served to further process the event as shown in Figure 6.1. The seven steps or phases in CISD are: introduction, fact, thought, reaction, symptoms, teaching, and re-entry.

Introduction

This phase allows the debriefing team to identify who they are, why they are there, what the group can expect, and what the ground rules for the debriefing are. It also motivates the participants and encourages mutual help.

The team introduces themselves, then shares information such as:

- Debriefings lessen the impact of the event
- People who go through a debriefing will eat/sleep/rest better
- Not a critique, not psychotherapy
- No notes or recordings are allowed
- Confidentiality is a must
- No one has any rank in the session
- Speak for yourself

- Ask questions any time you wish
- No breaks
- Everyone belongs here?

Fact Phase

This is the step developed to get people talking about the event. The team asks:

- Who are you?
- What was your role in the event?
- What happened from your perspective?

This step usually clears up some of the physical aspects of the incident, and the group has a much clearer picture of what happened during the incident.

Thought Phase

This step gets people to discuss personal issues, by identifying what they were thinking about. This is a transitional phase between what they did and what they felt, and from the cognitive domain to the emotional domain. They are asked:

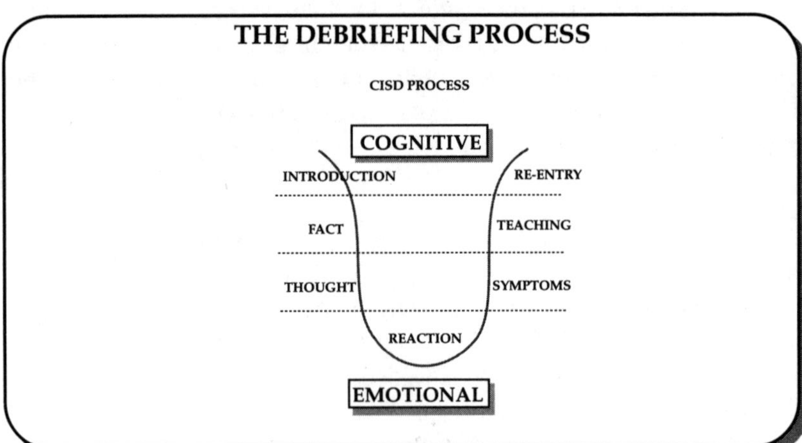

Figure 6.1 The Debriefing Process illustrates the cognitive - emotional - cognitive flow during the CISD process.

From *Critical Incident Stress Debriefing: An operations manual for CISD, defusing and other group crisis intervention services* (3rd ed.) by Jeffrey T. Mitchell, Ph.D., CTS and George S. Everly, Jr., Ph.D., CTS, p. 166. Copyright 1997 by Chevron Publishing Corporation. Reprinted with permission by the author.

- What was your first thought or most prominent thought once you got off "auto pilot" or once you really realized what was happening?

This leads the group into the most powerful phase of the debriefing, identifying their emotions.

Reaction Phase

This phase asks the participants to look at the entire event, and then identify what bothers them the most. They are asked:

- What is the worst part of this event for you personally?
- What feeling (emotion) does that evoke?

Other variations of this phase question are:

- If you could erase one part without changing the outcome, what would it be?
- What aspect of the situation causes you the most pain?
- What do you think will stick with you most?

Symptoms Phase

This is the transitional phase used to begin to move the group back from the emotions of the event to the cognitive portion of the intervention. Participants are asked:

- How do you know this event is having an effect on you?

Team members may prompt the group with cognitive, behavioral, emotional, physical, or spiritual questions. Prompting could include:

- What was it like for you at the scene?
- What was it like for you a few days after the event?
- Any leftover symptoms now?

Teaching Phase

This phase aids in bringing the group back to the cognitive level. The team members now are active in identifying that all of the group members' reactions and symptoms are normal and natural reactions to having experienced an unnatural event. They first communicate to the participants all the information that was shared with them, identifying the normalcy of those reactions and identifying what they can do to alleviate the reactions. They also advise:

- Do not fight it—give it time
- Watch your diet
- Be careful of stimulant intake
- Balance out your work, rest, and play
- Be aware that help is available
- Seek support and help from others
- Maintain your routine

Re-entry Phase

This is the final opportunity to lock the group into the cognitive and away from the emotional reactions to the event. The team will clarify what was shared, answer questions, make summary statements, and assist the group in developing a plan of action for the group or individuals as fits the scenario. The team covers the following:

- Asks for additional questions
- Asks if there is more to discuss
- Encourages the group to develop a plan of action
- Reminds the group of confidentiality
- States that the team will be around after the debriefing for as long as needed
- Provides handouts for group members
- Remains available for further services if the participants wish or have need

The debriefing team stays on site as long as there are people that want to talk. Then they have their own debriefing. CISD teams debrief themselves after every debriefing because they have heard and shared things which have affected them. They need to vent the emotions they have experienced prior to returning to their workplace or home.

Individual Interventions

The ICISF model of individual intervention is the SAFE-R model (Everly & Mitchell, 1999, pp. 76-80). This was developed by George Everly to address the aspects of working one-on-one with emergency workers. It is structured in such a way as to be adapted for use with other individuals as well. This five stage SAFE-R model is summarized in this section.

SAFE- R Model

Stabilize the Situation

This is done to remove the person in crisis from the stressor and to mitigate affective escalation. It also allows for mental status assessment. This can be accomplished by the CISM team member saying something such as: "Do you need a break?" or "I need some information, could you help me?"

Acknowledge the Crisis

This is done so that the person in crisis can describe "what happened" and identify their personal reactions. This is done to encourage catharsis, reduce arousal, establish rapport, and provide a sense of safety. It also provides for cathartic ventilation. The CISM team member can ask them "What is happening with you at this moment?" or "What is the worst part right now?"

Facilitate Understanding

This is done so that the CISM team member can explain the symptoms the person is feeling, enabling them to view the symptoms in the context of survival mechanisms. One goal is to have the person realize that their symptoms are normal reactions although those reactions may be a potential problem. The CISM member may say, "These are normal reactions to an abnormal situation." Another goal is to assist the person in crisis to focus on the cognitive, not the emotional aspects of the incident. Asking "What will help you right now?"can refocus the person in from feeling to thinking.

Encourage Adaptive Coping

We encourage adaptive coping by teaching basic stress/crisis management survival skills to the person in crisis. This is done to improve their immediate and short-term coping, and to see if they can develop a plan for immediate use. The CISM person can share such statements as "Let it go, don't fight it" or "Talking about it helps" and "What do you plan (or what would you like) to do now?"

Restore to Independent Function or Refer

The CISM person must now assess whether the current adaptive functioning of the crisis person is adequate for them to return to their assigned duty, or if the crisis person may need to be referred for more assistance. Either the crisis person has reestablished psychological homeostasis or is in need of continued acute care.

The CISM person may say "Are you ready to go back to work?" or "Would you please come with me to another area."

Acute Traumatic Stress Management

Another one-on-one procedure, developed by the American Academy of Experts on Traumatic Stress, is called the Acute Traumatic Stress Management (ATSM) (Lerner & Shelton, 2001). Incidents will occur on campus where the ATSM model may work better than the SAFE-R model. This model was originally developed for paramedics, but is easily adapted to the college/university setting. There are ten specific steps to this model. The first four steps are *physical* first aid and will not be addressed here. The last six steps are *psychological* first aid, and are as follows:

- **Observe & Identify.** Who has been exposed and who is evidencing signs of traumatic stress?
- **Connect.** Engage the individual by refocusing (if necessary)
  —Distraction: introduce an irrelevant topic
  —Disruption of their emotional reaction: "take a deep breath"
  —Diffusion of emotional state: i.e., match their voice, speech, and pace, then control.
- **Ground.** Orient the victim by discussing the *facts* about the event, where they were, what they saw, heard, smelled; what they did; how their body responded. Discuss what they experienced, not how it *felt*.
- **Support.** Give back a sense of control through a facilitative and helping attitude. Realize, understand, and communicate an appreciation for their pain and suffering.
- **Normalize.** Normal person/abnormal event. Identify typical reactions; validate their responses.
- **Prepare.** Review the event, bring the person to the present, and describe likely events in the future. Encourage them to seek further help/provide referrals.

The ATSM process is more cognitively oriented and sometimes seems to address the issues (fit) of the victim in the college setting as well or better than the SAFE-R model.

The next portion of this chapter identifies the use of the interventions portion in the core components listed above, in specific situations that commonly arise in crisis interventions that call for the use of modification of the core components to fit the scenario.

Family Interventions

This section outlines strategic applications of some of the crisis intervention techniques described above.

Any crisis event that arises on the college/university campus will inevitably directly or indirectly affect the family of those individuals involved in the crisis. In each case, CISM persons may use any of the five interventions just presented in this chapter to alleviate the stress caused by the incident. A CMB, defusing, or one-on-one can be used directly as stated here. However, minor modifications will be needed when providing debriefings (Everly & Mitchell, 1999, pp. 89-91).

This difference is mostly in the semantics of the intervention, i.e., asking the *fact* or second step question a bit differently. For example, the team member would more likely ask "Where were you when you heard about the incident?" or "What were you doing when you received word of the incident?" instead of asking "What was your role in the incident?" The rest of the steps can be provided as stated here, as they will generically address any situation.

Organizational Crisis Interventions

This model is used in the business world for a great number of instances. For example, many debriefings have been provided when companies have down-sized; others when there has been a major accident at the building or plant. Interventions following shootings, suicide, robbery, and other traumatic incidents are common in the working world.

The interventions listed earlier can be directly applied in most circumstances. In those few where they might not be appropriate, a modified version of the group processes such as defusings and debriefings have worked very well.

Pastoral Crisis Intervention

Pastoral Crisis Intervention (PCI) has been defined by Everly (2000) as the functional integration of faith-based resources with traditional crisis intervention assessment and intervention technologies. In times of crisis, people seek out spiritual guidance. When incorporated into Critical Incident Stress Management, PCI provides a "value added" degree of intervention that is very commonly expressed during and following a crisis.

All the interventions listed previously are used in the Pastoral Crisis Intervention programs. Each is adapted to fit the group or individual being worked with, and each can be adapted through practice to provide the intervention needed. The special adaptations taught in PCI are in many cases based in the SAFE-R model, whether working with individuals or groups. Much of crisis intervention training in PCI is training in what *not* to do more than it is what to do. Potential problems include but are not limited to: failure to "listen" to secular needs of the person; attempting to explain theologically "why" a trauma occurred; preaching to the "unreceptive" individual; and attempting to "convert" the unreceptive individual (Everly, 2000, p. 71).

Pre-Crisis Interventions

Pre-crisis interventions, another of the core components, will be fully addressed in Chapter 7 of this book.

Follow-up and Referral

Follow-up and referrals are the last core components listed in the work and in textbooks addressing CISM. But being last does not mean they are the least important. None of the interventions listed in this chapter and in this book can be ethically provided if there is not specific follow-up provided for all affected personnel. A part of the description of any intervention includes that follow-up needs to be provided. In most cases, there is a 24-hour follow-up, then contact is made again in three days, then in three to six months, and one year (anniversary date) later. Experience has shown us that the 24-hour and one year follow-ups are the most important.

References

American Psychiatric Association. (1994). *Diagnostic and statistical manual of mental disorders* (4th ed.). Washington, DC: Author.

Everly, G.S. (2000). Pastoral crisis intervention: Toward a definition. *International Journal of Emergency Mental Health, 2*, 69-71.

Everly, G.S., & Mitchell, J.T. (1997). *Critical Incident Stress Management (CISM): A new era and standard of care in crisis intervention.* Ellicott City, MD: Chevron Publishing.

Everly, G.S., & Mitchell, J.T. (1999). *Critical Incident Stress Management (CISM): A new era and standard of care in crisis intervention (2nd Ed.).* Ellicott City, MD: Chevron Publishing.

Flannery, R.B. Jr. (1999). Critical Incident Stress Management (CISM) The Assaulted Staff Action Program. *International Journal of Emergency Mental Health, 1,* 103-108.

Lerner, M.D. & Shelton, R.D. (2001). *Acute Traumatic Stress Management: Addressing Emergent Psychological Needs During Traumatic Events. AAETS Publication.* Commack, NY.

Mitchell, J.T. & Everly, G. S., Jr (2001). *Critical Incident Stress Debriefing: An operations manual for CISD, defusing and other group crisis intervention services* (3rd ed.). Ellicott City, MD: Chevron Publishing.

CHAPTER 7

Pre-Crisis Plans: The Development of a Crisis Response Team

By Dan Casey, Ed.D.

Development of a Crisis Response Team on Campus

In today's world, it is easy to identify the need for crisis response teams in our colleges and universities. One has only to pick up a newspaper or turn on the television or the radio to hear about some traumatic event happening in a college or university in the region, country, or world.

Most campuses have a crisis management plan developed for their college or university. Most of these are large plans that are detailed, and finite, and that identify the activity needed to be taken for building security and safety, accounting of personnel, safe areas for escape depending upon the type of event, and perhaps a chain of command and a telephone tree for communications. Most of these plans do not address human factor information needed to assist the individuals who are overwhelmed emotionally by the event, as well as the survivors of a crisis event. This chapter is provided as a means to identify how to invoke human factor management into a campus crisis plan. We will designate this human factor information as a Crisis Response Team (CRT).

The steps in developing a CRT on campus vary according to the needs of each individual school. Most colleges can follow this guideline with a minimum of adaptation. The changes from the norm would be the needs of your specific college. For example, an all-female campus will respond to calls of a different nature than will a team at an all-male college. Thus, each team will share many of the same issues but there will be significant differences on each campus that will modify the overall crisis response team's activities and duties. An inner city college in Minneapolis would address much different issues than a college in a less urban settings.

The CRT consists of those individuals who react to and intervene in the crisis. The composition of the CRT must reflect the system it serves. This team has specific structure, roles, and positions. It can be structured on the National Interagency Incident Management System (NIIMS), any version of NIIMS, or a structure identified, developed, and used by the school/college system prior to the installation of a CRT.

The steps identified in this chapter are loosely based on guidelines identified in Critical Incident Stress Management (Everly & Mitchell, 1999) as well as the guidelines identified in the Basic CISM Course Workbook (Mitchell & Everly, 2001).

Step One: Identify and Determine the Need for a Team

Most CRTs develop from the counseling departments on college and university campuses. As they are usually the first to be called on to respond when a crisis event occurs, they are probably the group on campus most likely to know what has happened and what response is needed.

There are a number of issues to address before developing a team:

- How many events have occurred in the last five years in this institution/building/campus that were traumatic in nature?
- Were they natural disasters? (Is the institution in a "tornado alley?")
- Were they man-caused incidents? (Suicides, automobile accidents, gang violence?)
- What types of industry are nearby?
- Is there a potential for traumatic events to happen in those industries?
- How would that affect the campus and the students?
- What programs are in place today to address traumatic events?
- Are those programs adequate?
- Do these events occur more often at any specific time of the year?
- Have they been adequately dealt with, or would a CRT have added important, beneficial services?
- Would prevention measures that a CRT can provide have lessened the number of events or the impacts of the events?

As these questions are processed, it will become clear if a trained

CRT is needed and should be developed immediately. If the answers to these questions merit the development of a crisis team, move to the next step.

Another issue that will affect the decisions made in Step One includes identifying the trauma response teams that are available at the present time. Answers to questions such as these will add to the information necessary for sound decision-making processes:

- Does your community have a community response team formed?
- Are there crisis incident management services available to the emergency response teams in your area?
- Are they trained in the International Critical Incident Stress Foundation's (ICISF) Critical Incident Stress Management (CISM) system?

Step Two: Gain Support from Administration

The counseling center on campus (who will probably take the lead in this crisis plan development) in most cases answers to the Vice President of Student Affairs, or a vice president of like title. Initial support for this crisis response team would usually start in that office. While detailing the benefits of having such a team on campus, the counseling personnel can also identify studies that show positive results. For instance, persons who have experienced crisis events and had CISM services provided recovered faster, with less use of sick leave and staff turnover, than did those not using CISM (Hokanson, 1997; Flannery, 1998).

Presentations should be made to the psychology, social work, and nursing departments, as well as campus ministry, as this would bring the subject into conversation at different levels and in different areas. This would also identify other mental health professionals who may become part of the campus CRT.

Once the vice president is convinced that developing a crisis response team is a good idea, you have opened the door for development of your specific team. Now, you may inform the vice president how much money and time are needed to provide the initial training and set up of the crisis response team.

Step Three: Form a Task Force to Develop the Team

This task force should consist of persons from every level of service on campus. There should be representatives from campus security, power plant, groundskeeping, faculty, staff, administration, and the student body. Each of these entities plays a part in any crisis that occurs, and each has its own specific methods of operation and deployment. Each brings its special CISM needs to the task force meeting. This task force has certain responsibilities. The following items are assignments that the task force will address.

Goals of the Crisis Response Team

The goals of the school CRT may include:

- Providing and maintaining a course or courses of action in the event of exposure to crisis incidents in the college or in actions that affect the college's members
- Providing education on trauma intervention to all members, both basic training and ongoing "in-service" training
- Making both the physical and emotional safety of individuals a priority
- Providing a preconceived plan of action that carefully assesses each step of the plan before it is enacted
- Making rapid assessments of student and staff needs
- Planning and carrying out appropriate interventions
- Using individual and group strategies
- Meeting special problems as they arise
- Assuring membership across the continuum so that all facets of the organizational population are addressed

Objectives of the Crisis Response Team

Along with goals, each CRT needs to develop objectives. An example of CISM objectives are these developed by Towson State University (Bennett, 1998):

1) Increase the effectiveness and immediacy of response to victims
2) Reduce the severity and duration of the trauma to the campus community
3) Reassure the public and local community
4) Guard the institution's image
5) Provide maximum preparation to reduce the potential for injury or damage
6) Provide a coordinated interdisciplinary and comprehensive response to a crisis situation
7) Facilitate assistance to primary, secondary, and tertiary victims
8) Provide coordinated internal and external communications

9) Facilitate coordination with external agencies
10) Prepare for post crisis support, evaluation, and condition

Team Membership Selection Criteria

Team member selection should start with requesting volunteers from each of the areas and positions mentioned previously. Volunteerism on the part of participants seems to be the largest reason the members remain in the organization.

One of the best methods to identify these volunteers is to have someone who is *really* interested, or persons who have been mandated by their institution, to attend a two-day basic CISM training. These trainings are available from trained trainers of the ICISF. Those persons trained will be the focus around which the entire CRT organization will be built.

Team membership personnel delineate guidelines for team membership and specific roles to be performed, including sending out and reviewing applications for membership on the CRT.

Towson University, Towson, Maryland, has formed a trauma response team. For team selection criteria, their proposal (Bennett, 1998, p. 13) stated "The Trauma Response Team will consist of trained professional (mental health and clergy) and peer (student, faculty, and staff) volunteers. This cross sectional approach of the team members is intended to provide a diversity that is reflective of the campus community for the purpose of appropriate peer representation during the actual crisis debriefings. Peer representation from all departments on campus will be solicited to volunteer as applicants. Several key departments in the Division of Student Life will form important links to the delivery of this crisis management service. These departments may include: university policy, residence, student health, nursing, campus ministry, athletics, office of students with disabilities, multicultural affairs, multicultural student life, and student development."

This statement reflects the fact that Towson University addressed their entire campus with team member selection. They based their team member selection criteria on the university's specific background and needs. The plan will arrange for and provide the basic CISM training necessary for start-up of the CRT.

Leadership

Once the decision is made to develop a CRT, the decision must be made as to who will bear the responsibility to organize and manage the team, as well as who will serve as coordinator or team director. A decision as to which staffing group will have the primary responsibility of coordinating all functions of the CRT must be made. Most campuses delegate this responsibility to either the counseling center or the Vice President of Student Affairs. In a few national circumstances the position of coordinator is farmed out to a mental health provider trained in the CISM concepts.

Legal Issues

Legal issues are an item pertaining to CRT development and are usually addressed within the school or university legal structure. There are no circumstances under which CRT personnel should circumvent legal counsel, campus policies and procedures, or their own professional judgment in their urgency to meet human need during crisis.

This is also the case for legal constitution of the CRT. These teams must be developed under the guidelines and structure of the sponsoring organization. Exploring liability issues and taking them into account when formulating team policy, procedures, and training will further assure legal boundaries are not exceeded.

Develop a Plan Funding for the Crisis Response Team

Funding for operations and training of team members will constitute a major portion of the initial funding needs of the team. Ideally, specific funding will be mandated by the highest power in the organization. Permanent funding, which is renewed annually, will assure the future of the team or teams.

Many colleges have requested and received grants for assisting in the initial set up of the CRTs, and others have been and are being funded annually by other grants requested to maintain the teams. Initial (one time) funding from life safety, residence life, and student affairs budgets on the campus, has paid for much of the college training that has been accomplished to date. Ongoing training and monthly meeting costs are usually shared by the counseling center, the mental health departments, and residence life funds. In some colleges, the student peers have formed a CISM club and have been granted club status and operating funds from student funds.

Step Four: Delineate Team Membership Roles and Guidelines

Administrative Structure

The norm of the administrative structure pertaining to disaster management in the higher education system at the present time is varied.

Many universities have appointed persons to be "disaster coordinators" or "emergency action personnel." These are members of the organization who have shown an interest in disaster management and have attended some type of disaster intervention training. Some are volunteer firefighters or volunteer medical technicians in their private life and have received training through those organizations. Many colleges and universities have asked the heads of the counseling department or psychology or social work faculty to be a part of or lead the system.

Director: Operationally, the Vice President of Student Affairs or the Director of the Counseling Center will best fill this role, as a team must have the highest organizational approval, and a director from this level will benefit the CRT team tremendously.

Coordinator: This position will be filled by a person who is thoroughly trained and experienced in the CISM model of crisis intervention, as well as having a very thorough knowledge of the system being served and its personnel. This position must also have ongoing support from and contact with all high level administrators to better address issues such as policy decisions, crisis response team needs, legal issues, and resource mobilization.

Crisis Response Team Leader: The team leader is responsible for maintaining a liaison with site administration, monitoring team operations and personnel functioning, providing redirection as necessary, and consulting the college management organization on an ongoing basis as needed.

Mental Health Professionals: School psychologists, school social workers, and health specialists usually fill this position initially. They form a strong element and the first line of defense when crises occur.

Staff, Faculty, and Student Peers: These are the "paraprofessionals" that influence the crisis intervention in a most productive way. These persons are trained in CISM techniques and are part of structured program that meets regularly to address issues and perform simulated exercises to assure they are ready when crises occur. To utilize the trust and preexisting relationships with those it serves, the CRT must have administrators, counselors, and teachers as part of this group also.

Referral Sources: Colleges and universities sometimes lack clinical expertise in crisis intervention. The need to locate and contact community resources, such as outside private and public mental health professionals. This is a necessary contact of each CRT. This can be accomplished either through actual team membership or through actual assistance contracts.

Each CRT, as it developed its protocols, identifies the mental health services available in its immediate vicinity as well as in nearby cities. These mental health resources will be available to all persons who were processed through the crisis intervention system. This information is a basic part of the CRT procedures manual and is updated annually to assure proper and timely referrals are made.

The CRT functions best under the direct supervision of the site administrator or his/her designate. Past experience has made it clear that in a crisis situation, the person filling the role of CRT leader must be someone who is not immediately involved in actual on-scene care giving, as distancing oneself from an incident provides a clearer perspective of the event and allows for better judgment to occur.

Step Five: Define Proper Practices of the Crisis Response Team

This step includes: Dispatching functions, response functions, activation for events, specific intervention techniques to be used, deactivation of the team-post event, follow-up after the response, and making arrangements for ongoing training.

Dispatching Functions

This issue is site dependent. If the institution has security or law enforcement personnel on site, such as many colleges and universities do, then the dispatching would usually be a function assigned to that group. If there are no such services available, then the dispatching will be accomplished from the administration site which has assumed this responsibility. Perhaps this will be a nearby city or village law enforcement office, or any other 24-hour service entity.

An example of how dispatching can be set-up is the following information about St. John's University, Collegeville, Minnesota. Let us suppose that a crisis event occurs on the campus or to any of the university personnel. The event is reported to life safety, the security office on campus that has personnel on duty 24-hours a day. The life safety dispatcher records all pertinent data on a form provided to them from the CRT's operations manual.

If requested by the reporting party the dispatcher contacts the CRT coordinator, who is listed on a form hanging above the dispatcher's desk. If the officer on duty foresees that emotional problems might arise from this event, they will contact the CRT coordinator regardless of whether assistance was requested by the reporting party.

The CRT coordinator (also a mental health professional in this case) makes the decision as to whether activation of the CRT will occur. Regardless of this decision, the CRT coordinator relays the information to the CRT director and to the college person they personally report to. The dispatcher's duty has been fulfilled by contacting the CRT coordinator and now he resumes his dispatching function. The CRT's organizational protocol should fully address the dispatching function, including the identification of persons by name and position and the specific role they will play in the dispatching.

Response Functions

This issue also reflects the system being served. If the incident affects students, then student peers are utilized in the intervention. If campus security is involved and affected, then the campus security peers are utilized as peers for the intervention. Mental health personnel are always utilized in any crisis incident on campus, regardless of the type of incident or peer action associated with the incident.

Activating the Crisis Response Team for Events

The protocol for activation of the CRT will be decided when the operations portion of the written plan and the manual are developed.

When a crisis occurs on campus, the security officer dispatcher will record all pertinent data, then contact the CRT coordinator and relay the information and possible request for CRT intervention. The CRT coordinator will review the incident, and make the decision as to whether or not the CRT is activated.

If the CRT is activated, the CRT coordinator will decide which of the seven components of CISM will be provided, as well as where, when, and by whom. The CRT coordinator determines what backup systems will be used in the case of mass disaster or wide spread communication failure. The coordinator will have, as part of the procedures manual, a list of all available off-site resources. This list will be activated at that time when it is decided that the incident requires more assistance than the in-house team can provide. In college and university systems, where the local CRT is overwhelmed or affected themselves by the incident, the team will have contact with other colleges or universities that have CISM teams available.

Minnesota has developed the Minnesota Intra-College CISM Network (MICCN), which provides immediate CISM services, both short and long term, for all colleges who are members in MICCN. One telephone number is available statewide that will activate CRTs from any number of colleges and universities as requested. The CRTs activated have mental health professionals, faculty, staff, and student peer members. Each entity has agreed to train and make available volunteers for the services described.

Specific Crisis Intervention Techniques

The specific intervention technique(s) used by the team (for example, defusing, CISD, or individual crisis counseling) will be decided by the team coordinator and team director.

The core components of CISM standard of care will be available as requested and needed. Depending upon the incident, the CRT may provide individual counseling, demobilizations, defusings, debriefings, on-scene interventions, family services, or referral to outside resources that will address the emotional aspects of the crisis event. These will be interventions that will identify issues pertinent to the group being addressed.

In addition, the CRT will have members present to address issues such as safety of personnel, security, accountability, notification of appropriate persons, communications, the media, funeral arrangements, and follow-up of the incident in both the short and long term.

Deactivation of the Team

In most cases the on-site coordinator makes the decision on deactivation for the specific incident. If that person is incapacitated, the CRT manager will request the decision from a constituent who will make that decision based on the information available.

Typically, when CRTs deactivate, this is accomplished with a minimum of decision-making criteria, as the circumstances are such that deactivation is the only appropriate action needing to be taken. In other cases, especially when outside teams are called in, the on-site coordinator will release the CRTs to return to their home base.

Follow-up for Team Members after a Crisis Response

Each team will debrief itself when coming off a crisis response call. This is a non-structured meeting held immediately after an intervention is provided. At this meeting, discussion of the intervention, as well as how other team members perceived both the event and their own reactions to it, is accomplished. The discussion also includes issues that may have come up between team members that could not be addressed while conducting the intervention, as well as discussion of other team members' perceptions of their peers.

The entire CRT will hold a second meeting of all team members to critique the incident, their role in it, the outcome, and plans for the next incident or the next training session.

Make Arrangements for Ongoing "In-Service" Training

The criteria for membership shall outline the amount and structure of the ongoing training that will be taken. In addition, each team will, from time to time, come upon incidents for which they have had very little training. When this occurs, it is beneficial to all team members to receive training in that particular incident and to critique the incidents in full for the benefit of all concerned.

Individuals should be required to attend basic and advanced CISM training if they have not been involved in CISM projects previously.

Step Six: Develop and Use a Clear, Practical Operations Manual

This manual will contain procedures, guidelines, and practices, and will address all the aforementioned issues. It will include all the forms to be used, the contract that all personnel have signed, and in-depth data on each type of intervention provided by the CRT. It should include background information about the team and describe the constituency it serves in a manner which clarifies the actions of the CRT.

A typical outline for the operations manual will include, but not be limited to:

- Acknowledgments
- Introduction
- Mission Statement
- Administration: Clinical Director, Program Coordinator
    - Team Coordinator
- Assistant Team Coordinator
- Lead Agency
- Team Training
    - Personnel Qualifications
    - Personnel Responsibilities
    - Membership Process
    - Team Membership/Length of Service
    - Revocation of Membership
    - Confidentiality
- Team Activation
- On-Scene Support Services

- General Information/Guidelines
- One-on-one Support Services
- Advice and Counsel to Command
- Assisting Victims, Survivors, and Families
- Demobilization Services
- Defusing
- Formal Debriefing
  - Common Questions
  - Pre-Debriefing Activities
  - Introductory Phase and Remarks
  - Fact, Thought, Reaction and Symptom Phases
  - Teaching, Re-entry and Post-Debriefing Activities
  - Additional Debriefing Considerations
- Follow-up Services
- Individual Consult
- Specialty Debriefings
- Initial Discussion
- Referrals Listing
- Appendix 1
  - Flow Chart
  - Structural Positions
  - Crisis Response Team
    - —Director
    - —Team Coordinator
    - —Referral Sources
    - —Team Leaders
    - —Team Members
    - —Mental Health Professionals, Staff, Faculty and Student Peers
- Appendix 2
  - Incident Specific Action
  - Site Coordinator Notified
  - Administration Personnel Notified
  - CRT Personnel Activated
  - Intervention Techniques Implemented
  - Referral System Implemented
  - CRT Calls Other Resources as Needed
  - Follow-up: Plans for the Future

Case Study:
Using the CISM Team on the University Campus

This is a story about an event that happens more often on campuses than most colleges and universities care to admit. It was a situation where activation of a CISM team was timely, well used, appropriate, and well received. There had been a CISM team on campus for about three years prior to this event, and the CISM had been very active on many occasions previous to this occurrence.

Rape On Campus

It is J-Term at a small university in a Midwestern state. J-Term is the time of year students catch up on the drinking they think they missed out on during first semester. J-Term starts the first Monday after January 1, and goes for three weeks. Students are required to enroll in one course during J-Term, which leaves a lot of time to accomplish their planned drinking catch up scheme (J-Term no longer occurs on this campus as of 2004).

By the end of the third week of J-Term, the parties start early and end late. This is the story of one of those parties. A second-year female student was introduced to a fourth-year male student. They met on Friday evening at the campus bar. He had been drinking for a while; she did not drink alcohol at first. They talked and got along pretty well. After an hour or so in the bar, she decided (after some coaxing) to have a wine cooler. She liked the taste and had a couple more.

By midnight, they had danced together quite a bit, and she started to get light headed. She decided she would go outside; since it was below zero, she thought the cold air would clear her head. She then came back in from the outside to find the male student waiting for her by the door. They embraced and kissed, then to cool *him* off, she asked if he would like to see the rest of the building that the bar was in. He agreed that he would. They toured the lower level, then got into the elevator to go to the second level. As the elevator doors closed, the male student started to tear off her clothes. Since he was twice her size, her resistance to this action hardly slowed him down. He tore off her outside garments and her bra, then took down his pants and raped her, tearing her panties in the process. She fought back as much as she could, and she screamed, but to no avail. They were in a deserted part of the building. When he completed his attack and rape, he tried to help her find her clothes. She screamed at him to leave her alone and he left.

She was hurt, wounded, bleeding, and sore. He had bruised her inside, as well as caused floor burns from the rug, and her head had been banged against the wall while he bounced on her. Her clothing was in tatters and she could barely move. She finally managed to cover herself sufficiently to leave the elevator and she went outside. By this time the busses were no longer in service, so she had no way to get back to her apartment/dorm room.

She held a work-study position at the campus ministry office, which was a short distance from the bar. She knew some of her workmates would be on duty there, so she hobbled over to campus ministry. Her workmates let her in, heard her story, and contacted the campus security people. They in turn called the county sheriff's office. They dispatched a deputy sheriff to the campus ministry office. After hearing her story and taking pictures of the bruises, cuts, and abrasions, the deputy gave her a ride to the nearest hospital. She was admitted and inspected by doctors and nurses trained in rape cases, then finally allowed to shower. After the shower, she was taken to the sheriff's office, where she was detained for four hours while they listened to her story, fingerprinted her, and had her write down all she could remember. She was then told she was not considered a victim by them; she was considered a witness.

The sheriff's office released information to the media about the "alleged" rape. Within two hours, satellite dishes from all three major networks were set up on the campus square. Any and all students that ventured near the square were questioned, cajoled, insulted, and asked asinine questions. This, of course, caused a great furor on campus and in the nearby cities.

The author had just completed teaching a 30-hour J-Term stress management course that included the 16-hour basic training for Critical Incident Stress Debriefing. One of the male students attending my course held a work-study position at campus ministry. He called me at home (Saturday) and informed me of the rape and its circumstances. He also said that he felt the campus CISM team should provide a debriefing to the persons who worked at campus ministry as they were all having a rough time following the rape. The group included 16 persons, both male and female workers, as well as the full-time staff of the campus ministry program.

We set up a debriefing for Sunday night, approximately 40 hours after the rape had occurred. It was attended by all 16 co-workers from the campus ministry program. We led them through the seven steps of the debriefing process. After 2½ hours, they were able to vent their feelings and discovered that others felt the same way. They recognized that they were not going crazy—just having natural reactions to an abnormal situation.

The campus was inundated with parents worried about their children. Many of the parents took their children home, as J-Term was over and there was a week with no classes. Crisis management briefings were offered during the next few days and were attended by over 200 family members. When second semester started the school held rallies and gave testimonials about the rape. All this added to or continued the media coverage for about three weeks after the incident. The campus finally quieted down and our CISM team did separate debriefings for the administration and for the people on the dormitory floor where the victim lived. They also hosted a walk-in discussion about the rape for anyone who needed to talk about it.

This case study shows that any incident that occurs on campus has the potential to distress individuals sufficiently to overwhelm their normal coping mechanisms and merit crisis intervention techniques.

References

Bennett, S., & Taylor, D. (1998). A proposal to develop a trauma response team at Towson University. Unpublished raw data.

Casey, D., & Leger, E. (2000). *Rural emergency response: A guide to coping with stressors in emergency services delivery* (2nd Ed.). Becker, MN: CMCC.

Everly, G., Jr., & Mitchell, J. (1999). *Critical incident stress management: A new era and standard of care in crisis intervention*. Ellicott City, MD: Chevron Publishing.

Hokanson, M. (1997). *Evaluation of the effectiveness of the critical incident stress management program for the Los Angeles County Fire Department*. Los Angeles: LACoFP.

Mitchell, J. & Everly, G.. Jr., (2001). *Critical incident stress management: The basic course workbook.* (3rd Ed.) Ellicott City, MD: Chevron Publishing.

Spivack, J. (1998). Towson university crisis response protocol. Unpublished raw data.

CHAPTER 8

During the Crisis

By Dan Casey, Ed.D.

This chapter will look at college and university methods of reacting to crisis situations. It will examine what happens on campuses without Critical Incident Stress Management (CISM) services, and how that differs from those campuses with CISM services.

Background Information

Let us suppose that a campus has experienced a catastrophic event. It is Friday, February 21, and the campus is three weeks into the spring semester. This campus (we'll call it Woebeset University) has a total student body of 4,000 students. It is a university where 80% of the students live on campus in dormitory-style housing. The male students' dormitories are on the south side of the campus; the female students' dormitories are on the north side of the campus.

There has been a fire on the top floor of a three-story dormitory on the south (men's) side of the university. Five persons perished in this fire. Four of these were third-year students; the fifth was a fourth-year resident assistant for the floor. Three of those dead were male students that had resided on the floor; the fourth was the girlfriend of one of the male students that perished. The fire started at 2:00 a.m.

Who's in Charge?

The president of the university is always in charge of the university, and the CISM team typically fits as shown in Figure 8.1. But who is in charge of the incident?

The fire department and law enforcement agencies have set up an Incident Command System (ICS) based upon the National Interagency Incident Management System (NIIMS). There is an Incident Commander (IC) in charge of the incident, and as many staff persons as the IC determined were necessary to manage the incident. They are in charge of the fire, but not in charge of anything pertaining to the university. Once the incident is concluded, i.e., the fire out and the investigation completed, the ICS is demobilized and all personnel return to their regular duties.

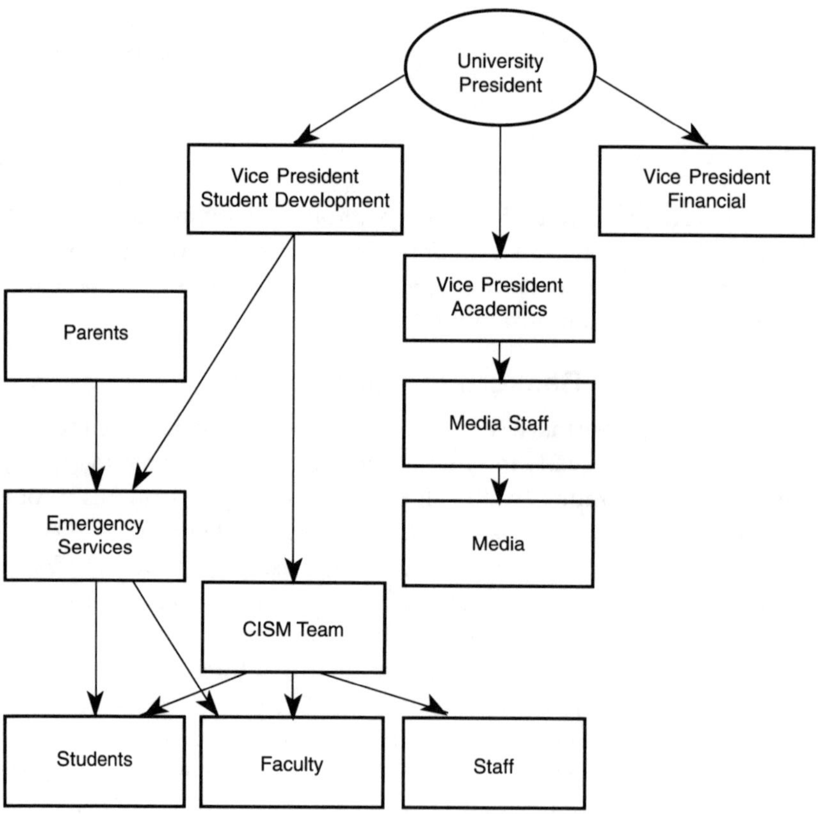

Figure 8.1 Typical college chain of command shows how the CISM team would configure.

Campus Reaction Without CISM

There is a campus crisis plan in place that was developed a few years ago, but no one has investigated to see if it addresses an event such as this, nor if it tells them what actions need be taken and in what order. It does not address the human factors portion of any incident other that to notify the personal counseling department.

It is now 12:00 noon. The fire has been extinguished and the removal of bodies has been completed by the fire department from the local rural city closest to the university. No one has been allowed on the scene of the tragedy since the fire and police departments ribboned off the area where the fire occurred. The campus law enforcement personnel have secured the area until the fire investigators from the state fire marshal's office arrive, and they have not appeared.

There are 40 students who live on the third floor of this building. All of them knew the victims very well, as they had been living together for six months by the time this fire happened. There is much crying and standing about in small and large groups, waiting to see what will happen next.

The Office of Public Relations is preparing a statement for the media. They are in the process of notifying the parents of the deceased students and reaching the parents of the unharmed students residing in that dormitory to assure them that their child is okay.

The Personal Counseling Center staff has been notified and three of the four counselors are on site at this time. They are overwhelmed by the event but are trying to work with those students who seem to be most disturbed by the event. They all knew these students and in fact, had been providing some personal counseling to two that perished.

The Campus Ministry personnel are on site and trying to help, but the director of Campus Ministry is on leave this week, and no one is sure what to do.

The floor resident (FR) of the floor that suffered this tragedy is on leave with the director of Campus Ministry, and there is very little dialog between the students from that floor and other FRs.

Communication

Who's talking to whom? Do the public relations persons know what is happening for sure, and does their media statement reflect the true state of affairs? Are they in touch with the campus security personnel so they know what they are doing? Have they any idea what the counseling department has been doing and if they have a plan to do anything else?

Notice that each of the entities on campus that should be involved is involved. They are each trying to do what they think best needs to be done from their perspective. However, they cannot see the whole picture because they are concentrating on their own small part of it, their normal reaction to an abnormal event. The problem is that there are many more persons (students, faculty, and staff) who are reacting to this than they are typically working with, and they are having reactions to it themselves.

Follow-Up Plan After the Fire Deaths

The floor residents and the resident assistants, as well as the instructors from each department have been asked by the personal counseling department to identify those students having difficulty with the situation and to send them to the personal counseling center. The counseling center is consequently overrun with people seeking assistance. By the end of second semester, two of the four personal counselors will have used a lot of sick leave and will not be providing the type of assistance needed to the students requesting help.

On Monday following the fire, the university's EAP was notified by the university president's office, and the EAP mailed flyers to each department identifying some of the things the instructors and staff who were impacted by the event could do for themselves; and they posted the EAP phone number on department bulletin boards. Since then they have been inundated with requests also.

The semester will end in June. Many students will still have not come to terms with their emotions over the fire incident, and leave for the summer frustrated and angry. Statistics show that 85% of the persons on campus were affected by this event, and that by semester's end, 5 to 15% of the student body, faculty, and staff are suffering from post-traumatic stress disorder.

Campus Reaction to the Same Event with CISM

This is the same scenario as listed before, the only difference being that the campus has had a CISM plan in place for two years. They have experienced a number of events, although no previous event held the magnitude of distress that this fire death incident evoked.

The fire occurred at 2:00 a.m. on Friday morning. The dispatch office of campus security received a telephone call. The dispatcher, a veteran of 8 years in campus security and 2 years as a member of the campus

CISM team, dispatched on duty officers to the scene immediately, contacted the director of campus security, then contacted the on-duty CISM team coordinator to inform that person of the incident and the fact that a crisis intervention program would need to be deployed. This dispatcher was able to accomplish this because pre-planning on the part of the CISM team had provided a charted form that the dispatcher filled out upon receipt of the information about the incident. This recorded information was then processed to the coordinator of the CISM team. Once the information was processed to the coordinator, the dispatcher had fulfilled his duty, and resumed the dispatching role.

The on-duty coordinator called the Director of Personal Counseling, who also happens to be the director of the CISM team on campus. The CISM director and coordinator together decided this was an event that would affect a large portion of the campus and that activation of the team was a necessity. A meeting of the director, coordinator, and key CISM team members was set for 7:00 a.m. Saturday morning. The on-duty coordinator went immediately to the dormitory where the fire had occurred to assist in whatever way possible. The coordinator also called a few student peers and one floor resident peer from the CISM team to meet them there. The coordinator met with the incident commander to see what he wished them to do. Then the coordinator and peers met together to assume specific roles at specific areas in the dormitory and on the campus grounds.

This consisted of working one-on-one with individuals who were severely affected by the event, and providing Crisis Management Briefings (CMBs) to groups of students and staff in order to keep the campus informed of what activities and services the university was providing and planning to provide. They also informed everyone there would be group sessions later on that day, and let people vent their emotions following the event. Some of the CISM peers stayed with affected individuals until later on that day.

At 7:00 a.m., a group of five individuals met in a meeting room in the square. This group consisted of the CISM director, team coordinator, two mental health professionals who are FRs and members of the CISM team, and one student peer. Action taken here was based on the pre-crisis plans as outlined in Chapter 7 of this book.

Plan of Action

An overall plan was adapted which included:

- Activation of the campus CISM team and a request to the vice president of Student Development that the telephone "bank," 15 of the office workers on campus, be activated to address incoming calls
- Defusings for small groups of affected persons
- Individual intervention for those most affected, immediately and over the next week
- CMBs immediately, and a daily schedule of CMBs for the next two weeks, so that all persons on the campus are kept informed of the plans and processes being offered by the university
- Debriefings (CISDs) starting on the following day, and more debriefings offered after the funerals
- Activation of other CISM teams from other colleges and universities to assist in the debriefings. Plans include defusing or debriefing of the debriefers before they leave the campus.
- Notification to mental health providers in the nearby towns who are trained in crisis intervention that they may be called upon to help
- Assignment of peer team members to specific duties, such as working with media personnel, liaison to food service, campus security, Campus Ministry, and the ICS organization
- Designation of a building on campus for the parents of the deceased who would soon descend on the campus. CISM mental health professionals, and Campus Ministry personnel would be assigned to work with them.
- Plans for a follow-up meeting of this group at 5:00 p.m. that day, and another in two days to set long-term plans for the CISM team
- Planned sessions for the home team CISM personnel to receive the interventions they need to survive this event

The CISM director then took this plan to the vice president of Student Development (his supervisor) to explain the CISM plan of action and to receive the authorization of those who will, in the end, most likely assume the expenses incurred. This is an essential step in the process, as it shapes everything else that happens on campus pertaining to this event. The vice president gave his okay to the plan and it was put into effect immediately.

The team coordinator then met with the incident commander of the emergency services organization to inform him of the plans of the campus CISM organization, and to offer assistance to their personnel if it was necessary.

Communications

As this university has its own television station (known on campus as the "blue screen") members of the CISM team quickly posted information concerning group meetings (CMBs) about the incident on the blue screen. Information as to events specific to the incident were only posted by the media relations personnel.

By 7:00 a.m., when the CISM team had their first meeting, the television satellites for all three major networks were set up on the square. This soon became one of the major headaches of the event, as rumors were rampant, and people were exposed to the worst rumors of the event. The CISM team members were warned to say nothing to the media, as it is the media relations persons who address this issue.

Follow-Up After the Fire Deaths—CISM Model

Individual interventions and CMBs continued all day, with the CISM team members taking as much personal time as they needed between interventions.

Defusings were provided to small groups of those affected personnel, with these groups being divided according to: (1) those students who lived and worked very closely with the deceased, and shared the same dormitory floor, (2) students who were living on other floors of the same dormitory, (3) classmates of these students, and (4) teammates from football, track, basketball, etc.

CMBs were provided for all dormitories on campus. At first the CISM team provided twice daily CMBs, then once a day after that in most dorms, dependent upon the needs of the residents.

Debriefings were offered starting on Sunday, approximately 48 hours after the fire occurred. These were offered using the same grouping criteria used for the defusings. Notice of the defusings and debriefings happened for the most part on the blue screen, and most dormitory floors had events boards to which notices were tacked. These notices identified the meetings as "chats" and invited everyone to attend, with a statement that there were a given number of spaces available at each session, so one needed to sign-up early to be guaranteed a spot at the "chat." As each dormitory had its own sign-up sheet, this provided its own limitations by site.

The funerals were completed by Tuesday, February 26. Another round of debriefings were scheduled starting on Thursday. These were offered to the same groups to whom the first debriefings were offered, and continued until all those affected were served. CISM teams from other colleges and universities conducted most of these debriefings. They came on campus in the order they were requested by the Woebeset CISM coordinator.

Debriefings were also given to faculty and staff of the college, with special emphasis on a debriefing for the president of the college and his staff, including the vice presidents of each area of the university. This debriefing was the hardest one to accomplish, as this group felt they did not need it and they did not have the time. It is specifically for those two reasons that the CISM team insisted on this debriefing because these people, who did the major decision making and answered to the media and the outside world, were as stressed or more stressed by the event as any student.

As the meetings of the CISM team continued, they addressed such issues as follow-up with affected personnel, memorials, anniversary dates, over the summer events, and any other issue affecting the human factors portion of the student body, as well as the faculty and staff.

It will be found through statistical analysis that less than 1% of the personnel involved in this crisis event suffered from posttraumatic stress disorder at the end of the spring semester, as opposed to the 5 to 15% of those who had no CISM crisis intervention techniques available.

CHAPTER 9

Crisis Intervention in the College and University Community: The Assaulted Staff Action Program (ASAP)

By Raymond B. Flannery, Jr., Ph.D.

Critical incidents are events that may disrupt an individual's usual and adaptive coping responses and may result in psychological trauma (Everly & Mitchell, 1999). The traumatized victim may experience disruptions in reasonable mastery, caring attachments to others, and a meaningful sense of purpose in life. If left untreated, posttraumatic stress disorder (American Psychiatric Association, 1994; Everly & Lating, 1995; Flannery, 1994a) may emerge. Victims may also experience symptoms of hypervigilance, exaggerated startle response, intrusive recollections of the event, and avoidance of the setting in which the event took place (American Psychiatric Association, 1994; Flannery, 1994a).

College and university students may encounter potential critical incidents during the entire course of their studies (Johnson, Ellison, & Heikkinen, 1989; Pledge, Lapan, Happner, Kivlighan, & Roehlke, 1998). Recurring critical incidents include homicide, suicide, sexual and physical assaults, domestic violence, natural and man-made disasters, riots, severe automobile accidents, HIV-AIDS, and other serious life-threatening illnesses [see reviews by Flannery (1995) and by Ottens & Fisher-McCanne (1990)]. University community victims may include traditional groups as well as women, persons of color, homosexuals, religious minorities, the physically challenged, and older faculty (Cerio, 1989).

The university community has a long and respected tradition of addressing student and faculty victim needs with crisis intervention approaches (Archer, 1992; Miller, 1995; Myer & Ottens, 1994; Ottens &

Fisher-McCanne, 1990; Pruett, 1990; Pruett & Brown, 1990; Thompson, 1990; Utterback & Caldwell, 1989). These interventions have primarily focused on one-to-one individual crisis counseling (Myer & Ottens, 1994; Pruett, 1990; Pruett & Brown, 1990), or group interventions by an interdisciplinary team representing various campus staff including the university counseling service, university housing, campus police, the administration, and the chaplaincy (Archer, 1992; Miller, 1995; Thompson, 1990; Utterback & Caldwell, 1989).

While student and faculty victims have been generally satisfied with these interventions (Ottens & Fisher-McCanne, 1990), these approaches have relied primarily on single interventions and there appears to be no empirical studies of the efficacy of these interventions with the university community.

Simultaneously, during this past decade, the field of crisis intervention has evolved from reliance on single interventions to multicomponent intervention approaches that are known as *Critical Incident Stress Management* (CISM) (Everly & Mitchell, 1999). CISM spans a continuum from pre-incident training through acute care interventions to post-incident response support. CISM approaches typically include individual crisis interventions, group and family interventions, and professional referrals. These approaches have been empirically demonstrated to be clinically efficacious (Everly, Flannery, & Mitchell, 2000) and are emerging as the international standard in emergency services care.

The purpose of this chapter is to outline an empirically validated CISM approach known as *The Assaulted Staff Action Program* (ASAP) (Flannery, 1998). Designed originally for employee victims of patient assaults, ASAP is flexible and modular and can be readily adapted to the needs of the collegiate and university communities.

ASAP: Theory and Philosophy

The Assaulted Staff Action Program (ASAP) (Flannery, 1998) is a voluntary, systems-wide, peer-help crisis intervention program for addressing the psychological aftermath associated with patient-to-staff assaults and other types of critical incidents. ASAP is a CISM approach that provides an array of services, each of which are based on the crisis intervention principles of immediate response; the gathering of facts; ventilation of affects; and restoring mastery, attachments to others, and meaningful sense of why the event occurred (Everly et al., 2000; Sandoval, 1985).

Each crisis intervention seeks to restore or instill in employee victims the characterization of stress-resistant persons (Flannery, 1994b). In previous studies of 1,200 persons over a twelve-year period, Flannery (1994b) identified six characteristics of persons who managed stressful life events adaptively. These characteristics included reasonable mastery of the environment; commitment to something of importance to the individual; healthy lifestyle choices of reducing the dietary stimulants of caffeine and nicotine, and adding periods of aerobics and relaxation exercises; social support; employing a sense of humor; and being concerned with the welfare of others. Since these characteristics may mitigate or prevent the onset of life stress associated with critical incidents, ASAP interventions emphasize the utilization of these skills.

The ASAP program is voluntary and employee victims may refuse services. It is systems-wide since victims often blame themselves for the critical incident to regain the illusion of mastery and might not come forward for assistance on their own. ASAP is based on the military principles from military medicine of proximity, immediacy, and expectancy (Grinker & Spiegel, 1945). The employee victim is treated at the site where the assault took place, as quickly as possible in the absence of serious medical injury, and with the expectation of remaining at the work site.

ASAP is guided by four basic assumptions. The first is that employee victims may experience severe psychological distress in the aftermath of violence. Second, employee victims are worthy of compassionate care. Third, talking about these events will mitigate or prevent the immediate stress associated with the event and result in more effective coping as well as minimize the development of lasting psychological disruptions in the longer term. Lastly, ASAP believes that, when critical events occur, it is not the employee's fault. Even if technical errors were made, the employee did not deliberately set out to cause the event. (True criminal behavior by employees is dealt with according to state legal procedures.)

ASAP has responded to physical assaults, sexual assaults, acts of verbal and nonverbal intimidation, sudden deaths of patients and employees, man-made disasters, and the like. All ASAP services are held in strictest confidence, have been approved by union and management representatives, and are provided as free employee benefits.

ASAP Structure

ASAP teams vary in size and composition based on the number of assaults per week in the facility, the number of worksites to be covered, the number of employees served, and the distance between worksites.

In large inpatient hospital facilities, ASAP teams are located on grounds; in community programs, ASAP teams are often mobile and travel between sites by automobile or van.

ASAP teams are interdisciplinary in nature and contain representatives from management, all clinical disciplines, nursing, and mental health workers. ASAP volunteers do not receive compensation for their services. However, if they respond to an incident off-shift, they are given compensatory time to be utilized within the subsequent thirty days. For purposes of illustration, an ASAP team for a four-hundred-bed hospital with eight hundred employees at fifteen different patient care worksites is presented. One episode of violence occurred in this facility daily.

The ASAP team for such a facility would include eleven first-line volunteer responders. First-line responders are on-call by page beeper for twenty-four hour periods once in every eleven days and one weekend monthly every three months. When a critical incident occurs, the first responder is summoned to the site by page beeper, offers ASAP services, and reminds the employee that all information is kept confidential, unless the employee reports a crime. (All employees, including ASAP team members, are mandated reporters of violence.) If the employee victim accepts ASAP services, the first-responder provides individual crisis intervention with additional follow-up by phone at three and ten days post-incident. First responders attend a weekly team meeting to review all cases and one monthly in-service training to enhance and maintain skills.

First-line responders are supported by three ASAP team supervisors who are also on-call weekly by page beeper. Supervisors provide second opinions as needed, provide individual crisis intervention in cases of multiple assaults, and assist with the group crisis interventions noted below. Supervisors attend all weekly team meetings and the monthly in-service training.

The ASAP team leader is responsible for the overall administration of the team and for monitoring the quality of services that are delivered. The team leader co-leads the group crisis interventions, chairs the weekly team meeting, ensures that all ASAP report forms are completed, provides for in-service training, and supports ASAP team members who may be victims of violence themselves by direct act, witnessing direct acts, or through vicarious traumatization (Flannery, 1994a; McCann & Pearlman, 1990). The team leader also monitors all ASAP team members for compassion fatigue (Figley, 1995).

ASAP Services

Consistent with the principles of CISM (Everly & Mitchell, 1999), ASAP offers a continuum of services that can be adapted to the various needs of facilities at different points in time. All employees are trained in the pre-incident techniques of alternatives to restraint and seclusion procedures to reduce the risk of assault. Should an assault occur, ASAP offers five crisis intervention procedures: individual crisis intervention, group crisis intervention, staff victims' support group, employee victim family crisis intervention, and professional referrals.

Individual Crisis Intervention

When an assault occurs, the charge nurse or clinical administrator at the patient care site is required to activate the ASAP program. The ASAP first-responder goes to the site, checks to be sure that safety and medical issues have been addressed, gathers the facts of what has happened, and offers services to the employee victim. If the employee victim accepts, the first responder assesses whether the employee has any disruptions in the domains of mastery, attachment, and meaning, as well as the symptoms commonly associated with traumatic events, especially hypervigilance, sleeplessness, intrusive recollections, and avoidance of the setting (Flannery, 1994a). As the victim recounts his or her understanding, the first-responder fosters ventilation of affects and empowers the employee victim by jointly reviewing how to restore mastery, attachments, and make some meaningful sense of what has happened. The same first-responder contacts the victim in three days and again in ten days to evaluate any further disruptions, symptoms, or need for additional ASAP services.

In cases where an assault occurs on site and the first-responder is off-shift, the first-responder contacts the site where the assault has occurred and speaks to the employee victim and the clinical administrator to see if the intervention should occur immediately or on the next day. If the need is immediate, the ASAP first-responder returns to the facility and completes an ASAP interview.

Group Crisis Intervention

On occasion, a particular assault or other act of violence involves multiple victims and disrupts the functioning of an entire campus. In these instances, ASAP employs the group crisis intervention procedure, Critical Incident Stress Debriefing (CISD) (Mitchell & Everly, 2001). This intervention is done with all community members present in group format. It includes a review of the facts of the incident; members' thoughts, feelings, and symptoms; and closes with basic strategies for victim coping. Again, the emphasis is on restoring mastery, attachment, and a sense of meaning about the critical incident (Flannery, 1994a). Group interventions are co-led by the ASAP team leader and/or one or more ASAP supervisors. The group interventions are always done in teams of at least two.

Staff Victims' Support Group

In some circumstances, additional support is needed. In those cases, the first responder refers the employee victim to the staff victims' support group. Co-led by the team leader and one ASAP supervisor, the group provides ongoing support to employee victims who need additional assistance in resolving the aftermath of the incident. Employee victims are given release time and paid the hourly wage to attend. The focus is on monitoring the presence of symptoms and restoring disruptions in mastery, attachment, or meaning.

Employee Victim Family Crisis Intervention

Some assaults on employees have an impact beyond the facility. This is sometimes true for the families of the employee victims, especially if they are single parents (Figley, 1989). In these latter cases, the children often fear becoming orphans and do not want the employee victim to return to work. In these cases, ASAP will meet with the family members to process the impact of the event on the family unit (Flannery, 1998).

Professional Referrals

From time to time, the present assault at the facility elicits memories in the employee victim of past episodes of violence in their personal lives. If these past events remain distressing to the employee victim, the employee is referred to a therapist who specializes in treating victims of psychological trauma.

With the exception of private counseling, all ASAP services are free of charge. ASAP information never becomes part of the employee's personnel file or medical record, and ASAP information is available from the ASAP team leader upon receipt of an ASAP release of information form signed by the employee victim. All ASAP team members are required to have malpractice insurance. This insurance is usually provided by the facility that hosts the team.

ASAP: Empirical Findings

From April 2, 1990, to December 31, 1999, there were 16 ASAP teams. Four teams were deactivated due to downsizing and privatization of health care services. There remained 12 teams on-line with over 200 ASAP team members. These teams were located in three states in state mental hospitals for adults and children, a private psychiatric hospital, community mental health centers, and community residential programs. These teams provided 395,800 hours of volunteer service to their various facilities.

Clinical Outcomes

ASAP responded to 978 cases of assault during the these 9 years. ASAP was accepted in 844 incidents and declined in 134 episodes (15% refusal rate). Mental health workers/residential counselors (69%) and nurses (23%) were more likely to be victims of assault. These assaults occurred during meal times in the hospitals and during the evening in community residences. Male staff (55%) were more likely to be victims of patient assaults than female staff (45%) The most common form of assault that ASAP responded to was physical assaults (88%) and the most common form of injury were bruises with swelling (48%).

As can be seen in Table 9-1, many employee victims experienced disruptions in the domains of mastery, attachment, and meaning. For many, these disruptions were restored within 10 days. Anecdotal evidence suggests that many victims also experienced symptoms of hypervigilance, sleeplessness, and intrusive memories. For most, the symptoms appeared to have resolved within 10 days.

Declines in Rates of Assault

An unexpected finding in the state mental hospital where the first ASAP program was fielded was a 62% decline in the rate of assault within two years (Flannery, Hanson, Penk, Flannery, & Gallagher, 1995). This

Table 9-1
Disruptions in Mastery, Attachment, and Meaning (N=844)

DOMAIN	INCIDENT	THIRD DAY	TENTH DAY
Mastery	61%	34%	19%
Attachment	36%	24%	16%
Meaning	58%	42%	26%

finding has been replicated in each of three additional state mental hospitals with a decline of at least 40% in each facility (Flannery, Hanson, Penk, Goldfinger, Pastva, & Navon, 1998); and in two community mental health centers with a decline of at least 25% in each facility (Flannery, Penk, & Corrigan, 1999; Flannery, Anderson, Marks, & Uzoma, 2000).

Dollar-Cost Savings

ASAP's ability to support employee victims remaining at work coupled with its decline in rates of assault have resulted in less human suffering, less medical and legal expense, fewer industrial accident claims, and sustained productivity. Each of these factors contributes to dollar-cost savings for each facility with an ASAP team. The original ASAP team in a state mental hospital saved its facility $268,000 over a two-year period in staff turnover costs alone (Flannery, 1998). [See Flannery (2001) for additional recent findings.]

Implications for Colleges and Universities

The ASAP findings to date (Flannery, 1998) appear to provide empirical support for CISM multicomponent approaches (Everly & Mitchell, 1999). The five ASAP component interventions appear to have been clinically efficacious in providing needed support to employee victims at a vulnerable point in their careers. For the majority of employee victims, disruptions in reasonable mastery, caring attachments, and a sense of meaning had resolved within ten days as had the presence of symptoms associated with acute stress disorder and PTSD (American Psychiatric Association, 1994; Flannery, 1994a). The replicated findings of sharp reductions in the rates of violence in several facilities after ASAP had been fielded further contributed to enhanced safety for both patients and staff, and, with fewer assaults occurring, reduced human suffering and medical and legal expense. These factors increased morale, sustained productivity, and suggest that a properly fielded ASAP program is a risk management strategy in its own right (Flannery, 2000). Thus, the psychological impact of critical incidents was both addressed in a timely fashion and reduced in overall frequency with important dollar-cost savings.

It is presently unclear why an ASAP program fielded *after* the critical incident should reduce the frequency of occurrence *before* these events take place, and research into the possible mechanisms for these declines is currently ongoing. First, it may be that ASAP empowers staff which, in turn, leads to improved morale and enriched quality of care. Employees may pay more attention to the early warning signs of violence and move to de-escalate these situations early on. Second, employee victims of repeated assaults may have developed avoidance responses to the patients and ASAP interventions may have addressed these previously developed avoidance symptoms with improved patient-staff interaction as an outcome. Third, as ASAP interventions are fielded, employees may perceive an enhanced level of support that reduces their anxiety. As their anxiety is reduced, the patients' level of anxiety may be reduced and the threshold for violence may be raised. A fourth possible understanding of these findings may be that the continuing presence of ASAP may be defining the employee victim as a true victim of violence and possible psychological trauma. This form of systematic redefinition of violence may modify the facility's culture of blame and enhance cooperative efforts to reduce violence. These or other possible explanations await experimental verification.

ASAP remains the most widely researched crisis intervention program in the world and is cited as a program of note in the federal Occupational Safety and Health Administration Guidelines (OSHA; 1996) for preventing violence in health care and social service settings. ASAP's empirical grounding and its flexible, modular structure would appear to provide college and university crisis intervention programs with a CISM approach of demonstrated clinical value.

ASAP and the University Community

ASAP (Flannery, 1998) appears to draw upon the strengths of previous collegiate programs by combining individual treatment interventions (Myer & Ottens, 1994; Pruett, 1990; Pruett & Brown, 1990) and group intervention initiatives (Archer, 1992; Miller, 1995; Utterbach & Caldwell, 1989) with additional helpful services for families and severely impacted employee victims. An ASAP team could be comprised of counseling center staff exclusively or an interdisciplinary staff with representatives from the various campus organizations that provide resources to faculty and staff. This team would then address the various potentially critical incidents that the university community may encounter (Flannery, 1995; Ottens & Fisher-McCanne, 1990). ASAP is flexible in its format so that it can be adapted to existing college and university team structures.

For example, in the case of a student suicide, the university crisis intervention team could be deployed to provide individual crisis intervention for those who found the body and for the deceased's roommate. A group CISD crisis intervention (Mitchell & Everly, 2001) could be held for other students in the dormitory. Family crisis counseling could be extended to the family of the deceased student and to other concerned parents. Additional support services for the university community could be provided as well as professional referrals, where indicated, to the university counseling center or nearby experts who specialize in counseling trauma victims. The crisis team could provide to the university community ongoing education about the possible signs of suicide risk as well as campus resources. This latter initiative would be a form of pre-incident training to reduce the risk of additional suicides in subsequent months.

If a community had a number of smaller colleges or community college campuses in near proximity, any one campus might not have the full resources needed to offer a fully comprehensive program. In these cases, a mobile ASAP program could be established. Each campus would contribute personnel for the crisis intervention team. The team members would train as one unit and then be deployed to any campus as critical incidents occurred.

ASAP programs of either a single or multi-site nature also provide the academic community with an opportunity to strengthen town-gown relations by being able to offer to the local community a crisis response team that could be activated for local critical incidents or disasters. A campus ASAP also provides the university with an excellent opportunity to work with and provide needed support to the local chapter of the Red Cross.

Fielding an ASAP Program

The design and fielding of a campus ASAP team can be completed in five steps with each step's tasks taking about one month to complete. (See Flannery [1998] for a more detailed review.)

The first step is to develop administrative support. Those interested in an ASAP team would meet with administrators, faculty, and the student body to provide information and assess needs. Meetings would also need to be held with representatives of professional associations or unions whose members might be involved. Legal issues such as ensuring confidentiality and malpractice coverage, as well as financial matters such as monies for on-call beepers and printing informational leaflets would need to be addressed. No ASAP program can function well without full senior administrative support.

The design of the team's size and structure is the second step. Included here are information on the actual or estimated number of occurrences within a month; the number of university faculty, students, and employees to be served; and the number of possible sites and distances between sites where critical incidents might occur. An average of four incidents per month in a university community of eight thousand on a two-hundred-acre campus would likely necessitate a team of approximately ten to fifteen members to provide adequate services without exhausting team members.

The third step is the selection of the team. The team leader is arguably the most important choice. ASAP teams run best when the team leader is versed in individual and group intervention principles, has good administrative and organizational skills, and is motivated to "own" the team. Team members should represent the necessary groups that campus life indicates. They should be interested in crisis counseling, have good interpersonal skills, and should understand the importance of confidentiality in delivering a clinical service such as crisis interventions. To ensure continuity, all team members should volunteer for at least a two-year period.

Next, the team needs to be trained in the structure and services of an ASAP program, the nature of critical incidents and psychological trauma, the principles of crisis counseling, and the general administrative procedures of how the team will function on its campus. These didactic presentations are interspersed with increasingly complex role-play examples of the various intervention skills to be mastered. This training usually takes a minimum of one and one-half days (Flannery, 1998).

Finally, the team is fielded. Announcements placed in dorms, student newspapers, and the like can provide a description of the team and its services and announce its start date. Informational meetings can be held by team members with various interested stakeholders in the university community. When the team begins, there may be some resistance to its utilization. Usually, these are fears about confidentiality and the victim's concern that he or she will be blamed for the event or be perceived as weak. Each ASAP team has encountered these resistance periods and has continued its work with those who were interested in receiving services. Each ASAP team has also encountered a subsequent defining event that impacted the entire facility. ASAP's supportive presence during this critical incident dissolved any subsequent resistance of note.

When the team is in place and providing services, it is the ongoing responsibility of the ASAP team leader to debrief team members after major critical incidents on campus (Mitchell & Everly, 2001) and to monitor team members for vicarious traumatization (McCann &

Pearlman, 1990) and compassion fatigue (Figley, 1995).

The psychological impact of critical incidents on faculty and students disrupts the college's and university's mission of the advancement of learning. ASAP (Flannery, 1998) would appear to provide the university community with a clinically efficacious, empirically grounded, cost-effective, risk management strategy for reducing suffering, increasing safety, and enhancing the mission of learning.

References

American Psychiatric Association (1994). *Diagnostic and statistical manual of mental disorders* (4th ed.). Washington, DC: Author.

Archer, J. (1992). Campus in crisis: Coping with fear and panic related to serial murders. *Journal of Counseling and Development, 71,* 96-100.

Cerio, N.G. (1989). Counseling victims and perpetrators of campus violence. *New Directions for Student Services, 47,* 53-63.

Everly, G.S., Jr., Flannery, R.B., Jr., & Mitchell, J.T. (2000). Critical Incident Stress Management (CISM): A review of the literature. *Aggression and Violent Behavior: A Review Journal, 5,* 23-40.

Everly, G.S., Jr., & Lating, J.M. (1995). *Psychotraumatology: Key papers and core concepts in posttraumatic stress.* New York: Plenum.

Everly, G.S., Jr., & Mitchell, J.T. (1999)., *Critical Incident Stress Management (CISM): A new era and standard of care in crisis intervention* (2nd ed.). Ellicott City, MD: Chevron Publishing.

Figley, C.R. (Ed.). (1989). *Treating families in stress.* New York: Brunner/Mazel.

Figley, C.R. (Ed.). (1995). *Compassion fatigue: Coping with secondary traumatic stress in those who treat the traumatized.* New York: Brunner/Mazel.

Flannery, R.B., Jr. (1994a). *Post-Traumatic Stress Disorder (PTSD): The victim's guide to healing and recovery.* New York: Crossroad Publishing.

Flannery, R.B., Jr. (1994b). *Becoming stress-resistant through the project SMART program.* New York: Crossroad Publishing.

Flannery, R.B., Jr. (1995). *Violence in the workplace.* New York: Crossroad Publishing.

Flannery, R.B., Jr. (1998). *The Assaulted Staff Action Program (ASAP): Coping with the psychological aftermath of violence.* Ellicott City, MD: Chevron Publishing.

Flannery, R.B., Jr. (2000). Post-incident crisis intervention: A risk management strategy for preventing workplace violence. *Stress Medicine, 16,* 229-232.

Flannery, R.B., Jr. (2001). The Assaulted Staff Action Program (ASAP): Ten year empirical support for Critical Incident Stress Management (CISM). *International Journal of Emergency Mental Health, 3,* 5-10.

Flannery, R.B., Jr., Anderson, E., Marks, L., & Uzoma, L.L. (2000). The Assaulted Staff Action Program (ASAP) and declines in rates of assault: Mixed replicated findings. *Psychiatric Quarterly, 71,* 165-175.

Flannery, R.B., Jr., Hanson, M.A., Penk, W.E., Flannery, G.J., & Gallagher, C. (1995). The Assaulted Staff Action Program (ASAP): An approach to coping with the aftermath of violence in the workplace. In Murphy, L.R., Hurrell, J.J., Jr., Sauter, S.L., & Keita, G.P. (Eds.): *Job stress interventions.* Washington, DC: American Psychological Association.

Flannery, R.B., Jr., Hanson, M.A., Penk, W.E., Goldfinger, S., Pastva, G.J., & Navon, M.A. (1998). Replicated declines in assault rates after implementation of the Assaulted Staff Action Program. *Psychiatric Services, 49,* 241-243.

Flannery, R.B., Jr., Penk, W.E., & Corrigan, M. (1999). The Assaulted Staff Action Program (ASAP) and decline in assault: Community-based replication. *International Journal of Emergency Mental Health, 1,* 19-21.

Grinker, R.R., & Spiegel, J.P. (1945). *Men under stress.* New York: McGraw-Hill.

Johnson, R.W., Ellison, R.A., & Heikkinen, C.A. (1989). Psychological symptoms of counseling center clients. *Journal of Counseling Psychology, 36,* 110-114.

McCann, L., & Pearlman, L.A. (1990). *Psychological trauma and the adult survivor: Theory, therapy and transformation.* New York: Brunner/ Mazel.

Miller, R.S. (1995). Largest earthquake at an American university, January, 1994: University counseling perspective. *Crisis Intervention and Time-Limited Treatment, 1,* 215-223.

Mitchell, J.T., & Everly, G.S., Jr. (2001). *Critical Incident Stress Debriefing : An operations manual for CISD, Defusing and Other Group Crisis Intervention Services* (3rd ed.). Ellicott City, MD: Chevron Publishing.

Myer, R.A., & Ottens, A.J. (1994). Assessment for crisis intervention on college campuses. *Crisis Intervention and Time-Limited Treatment, 1,* 31-46.

Occupational Safety and Health Administration (1996). *Guidelines for preventing workplace violence for health care and social services workers.* #3148. Washington, DC: OSHA Publications Office.

Ottens, A.J., & Fisher-McCanne, L. (1990). Crisis intervention at the college campus center. In A.R. Roberts (Ed.), *Crisis intervention handbook: Assessment, treatment, and research.* Belmont, CA: Wadsworth Publishing.

Pledge, D.S., Lapan, R.T., Happner, P.P., Kivlighan, D., & Roehlke, H.J. (1998). Stability and severity of presenting problems at a university counseling center: A 6-year analysis. *Professional Psychology: Research and Practice, 29,* 386-389.

Pruett, H.L. (1990). Crisis intervention and prevention with suicide. *New Directions for Student Services, 49,* 45-55.

Pruett, H.L., & Brown, V.B. (1990). Crisis intervention and prevention as a campus-as-community mental health model. *New Directions for Student Services, 49,* 3-16.

Sandoval, J. (1985). Crisis counseling: Conceptualizations and general principles. *School Psychology Review, 14,* 257-265.

Thompson, R.A. (1990). Strategies for crisis management in the schools. *National Association of Secondary School Principals Bulletin, 74,* 54-58.

Utterback, J., & Caldwell, J. (1989). Proactive and reactive approaches to PTSD in the aftermath of campus violence: Forming a traumatic stress outreach team. *Journal of Traumatic Stress, 2,* 171-183.

CHAPTER 10

Summary Chapter – Epilogue

By Dan Casey, Ed.D., and Judith Putzel Price, Ed.D.

It has been four years since Russ Lee and Dan Casey met to talk about the need for college and university trauma response guidelines. They decided they needed to develop a book on the subject. The plan that developed was to access people in the crisis field who were experts in their specific areas, and who would put together a chapter on their specialty. It worked!

The stories are true. The lessons learned are clear and provide an avenue for interventions that bypass cultures, languages, and borders. Suffering and loss are inevitable elements of life.

The events that occur on campuses around us every day, making headlines in the news, verify the need for appropriate and effective intervention strategies. On college and university campuses in the last few months, there have been suicides, death by fire, automobile deaths, and countless injuries due to alcohol abuse. Many sites have a workable crisis response plan; but in truth, many more do not. Most colleges and universities that we have been called in to work with have a plan that tells them where to shut off a given switch, who to call when a certain type of event happens, and which building to evacuate, and when. Almost all the plans provide a good overview of what needs to occur when a catastrophic event occurs. Where almost all of them fall short is planning for the needs of the people affected by this event. Their plan tells who they call to stop the bleeding, but falls short when addressing the psychological and emotional reactions experienced by those involved, as well as those that saw it happen or had a close friend or relative involved. In many cases this entire issue is addressed in a statement such as, "the counseling center has been notified" or "those needing to talk about the event were sent to the counseling office." In many instances the counseling office personnel are personally involved in the incident already, perhaps on site, counseling some of those affected, or had friends involved. This also does not address the crisis intervention training that the counseling group may or may not have had.

The purpose of this book is to address that part of a crisis. Once a traumatic incident has occurred, there is a finite set of phases or steps that need to be followed to assure that all of those affected by this event have been given an opportunity to discuss the event, vent emotions about the event, and hear some basic guidelines to help them effectively process the event.

The case study of the tornado that touched down at Gustafus Adolphus College in St. Peter, Minnesota, was the opening chapter of this book. It provided a very succinct overview of crisis response on a college campus that drew assistance from many areas and was the catalyst for development of the Minnesota Intra-College CISM Network (MICCN). It gives a good overview of how CISM works, and how it can be adapted to fit any circumstance and group of people.

The description of traumatic stress disorders lays out the groundwork for the rest of the book, by identifying what we hope to prevent by making this information available to colleges and universities worldwide.

Vicarious traumatization (secondary traumatic stress or compassion fatigue) describes what can happen from exposure to another person's trauma. It addresses the etiology of symptoms and also identifies various avenues open to the college or university personnel for reducing the exposure and mitigating the impact that occurs following a crisis event.

Next we addressed the effects of trauma on post-secondary learning, identifying those reactions that students typically have following exposure to a traumatic event; what the results of those reactions are; and what we need to do to assist the traumatized student.

The discussion on working with parents of college and university students identifies reactions an organization can expect to see the parents experience and the best things to do for them. By defining the rights and limits of privacy and the release of information, a very clear guideline is provided on what colleges and universities need to do to address these issues. Parents will feel more at ease with the situation and feel that the school is doing everything it possibly can for their child.

Chapter 6 leads us into the heart of the issue of crisis intervention on campus. It outlines and explains the core elements of CISM. It clarifies the specific crisis interventions used in the CISM model of crisis management. It addresses how each of these core elements are adaptable to college and university situations, and why they have been so successfully used in the past. Then, in Chapter 7, we go on to describe how the development of a crisis response team typically comes about on campus. We discuss the need for the human factors portion of crisis intervention, which is working with all personnel affected by any given crisis event, and how the development of a crisis response team and crisis response plan on campus alleviates most of the chaos following a crisis event.

The next chapter describes what happens during a crisis using two scenarios. The first is a college that has no workable crisis response plan. The second is the reaction to the same event by a college that has a working, viable crisis response team developed and available. The advantages of being prepared and using crisis intervention are clearly visible.

Chapter 9 addresses crisis intervention in the college and university community using the Assaulted Staff Action Program (ASAP). Raymond Flannery has outlined and demonstrated how the ASAP program can be utilized and incorporated into any campus program. The empirical findings provide information that shows the benefits of using the ASAP program. Flannery goes on to describe how to incorporate ASAP into the college/university community and what benefits the institution will reap by following the guidelines.

The Appendix provides role play scenarios for colleges and universities to use once they have a CISM team established. It provides well written scenarios to practice crisis intervention techniques. Any college or university can take these role plays and use them directly, or as outlines to model their own.

Our intention in developing this book was to provide a tool for crisis intervention that could be used directly in building and maintaining a successful crisis response team on any college or university campus. We wanted a hands-on, illuminated guide for actively developing and maintaining a crisis response team on any campus.

We feel that an important way of consolidating the information in this text and developing the skills of teams is to train for trauma.

APPENDIX

College and University Crisis Scenarios

By Dan Casey, Ed.D.

The following scenarios are some that we have used in CISM team training sessions since our first training in basic CISD intervention. Our recommendation is to hand out a scenario to a practicing team and have 5 to 7 people volunteer to do the role-play and 3 people serve as the team. Assigning specific roles is helpful, but not always necessary. We have found that the spontaneous roles that individuals select impart a freshness and element of the "unexpected" to the experience. Role-plays become very real. The kinds of feelings, situations, and interrelationships that evolve are similar to those that expected in a real life debriefing. One of the benefits of these role-plays is that when a real debriefing is necessary, the emotional levels of the team are not much greater than they were in the role play.

Scenario One

Construction work on campus caused an underground explosion that shot noxious gas into classrooms in Morrison Hall. Classes were in session and it was raining outside. Immediate panic ensued as everyone ran outside. Emergency vehicles arrived on the scene. A well-known and well-liked professor did not get out of her office in time and died of gas poisoning.

Intervention

A debriefing was offered the following evening for the students that were in the building when the explosion occurred, as well as some that were in the deceased professor's class.

Roles

Paul—A student. He was in history class on the second floor and the professor refused to let the class go right away, making them the last to get out of the building. His obvious anger covers the absolute terror he felt at the time.

Meg—A student. One of the first out, Meg stood out in the rain for at least an hour afterwards, too frightened to move. She was absolutely convinced that this was an attack by a terrorist, that the administration "doesn't know anything" and should be doing more to protect everyone from more terrorist attacks. She was unable to eat or sleep.

Jen—A student and trained EMT. She found herself running around trying to help and to calm students. She felt helpless and wished she could have done more.

Ben —A student and resident assistant in Huntress Hall, the building across the quad from Morrison Hall. Many of his residents were in class in Morrison at the time of the explosion, and he is finding it difficult to respond to them as they call him in fear of another explosion/ attack at all hours of the night. Their lack of sympathy for the deceased professor has upset him. Ben's own parents had been killed in a tragic car accident three months previously.

Mona—The deceased professor was her advisor. Mona struggles academically and is in a panic about what she will do without her advisor. She feels extremely guilty and ashamed that her first and frequent thoughts are about herself instead of her deceased professor. She has not slept since the incident and vomits whenever she tries to eat. She plans to withdraw from school.

Scenario 2

Brian was the incoming president of his fraternity. He and his friends were out drinking at a local bar the night before semester began. Brian had driven to the bar and wanted to drive back to the fraternity. Melissa, Jessica, Dylan, Jason, and Bob had been drinking with him. They tried to convince him to walk back because they all were inebriated, but Brian said that his computer and stereo were in the car and he did not want to leave them on the street overnight.

Brian, Jason, and Bob got in the car to drive back, while Dylan, Melissa, and Jessica walked home. On the way home Brian ran a stop light, hitting another car. Brian was thrown through the windshield, taken to the hospital, and died in intensive care one day later. Bob had lacerations to his face having been thrown through the windshield also, and

Jason had a broken arm. Both were released from the hospital within 24 hours.

Intervention

A debriefing took place two days after Brian's death. Participants in the debriefing were those persons involved that night as well as other fraternity brothers who were back at the fraternity house, heard the accident, and went out to the scene of the accident.

Roles

Bob—The type of student who does what anyone tells him, even if he does not think it is a good idea. He is often the designated driver because he does not like to drink, but on this night his friends had talked him into drinking more than usual.

Jason—The big partier, drinks the most, gets into fights all the time. Whatever anyone can think to do, Jason will think of a bigger, riskier way to do it. He had been urging Brian to drive faster.

Dylan—Dylan vacillates between being glad he refused to ride with Brian and deep grief. He was Brian's closest friend and had known him since childhood. He will probably be the new president of the fraternity.

Melissa—A member of the sister sorority, she had wanted to date Brian for the last year. They had finally hooked up the night before and she was going to meet him at the frat house later.

Jessica—Melissa's best friend. Her twin brother, also named Brian, was injured in a car accident a month before and is still in the hospital. Like Jason, Jessica parties heartily. She had a friend in high school who was killed by a drunk driver.

Scenario 3

Jack was a sophomore residing in Fiske Hall. He was an abrasive young man who lacked social skills, was somewhat cocky, and did not make friends easily. He did have a couple of friends with whom he played video games and "Dungeons and Dragons." There was one woman with whom he had begun to develop a close relationship, as she was learning that despite his tough exterior he was vulnerable on the inside. Jack returned from a weekend home to find that due to two major altercations on campus, he was being removed from campus housing. On Monday night Jack shot himself with a handgun. Students on the floor heard the shot. A roomer next door was the first person on the scene. The resident assistant called 911. Jack's roommate returned to find the EMTs working on Jack. Jack was taken to the hospital where he was pronounced dead.

Intervention

A debriefing was offered for students living in the resident hall. Another debriefing was offered for staff and for faculty. A general debriefing was attended by:

- Student EMS staff and the dispatcher who answered the call
- A building custodian who had talked with Jack that morning
- A member of the custodial staff/nurse who had to clean the room
- Security members who stood watch over the body until it was taken away
- Security members who cordoned off the dormitory so other students could not enter
- The counselor with whom he had an appointment
- A nurse with whom he had an appointment

Scenario 4

There was a fire in an off-campus fraternity house housing 15 students. The fire started after a night of major partying. Mark, John, Gary, and many others were also using drugs. Mark and John passed out. Gary fell asleep while smoking, starting the fire that swept quickly through the building. Firefighters found Gary (alive) in a room close to the stairs to the third floor. Mark and John, passed out in a back third floor bedroom, died in the fire. Other fraternity brothers escaped from the first and second floors. John was a graduating senior and was going to be married in June to Melissa. Several women had been partying with the fraternity brothers and suffered smoke inhalation.

Interventions

A five-step debriefing (Mitchell & Everly, 2001) was offered to the residents of both fraternity halls the morning following the fire, and a seven-step debriefing was provided two days after the second funeral.

Scenario 5

A psychology professor committed suicide. His death affected students, staff, and faculty.

Interventions

CISDs were offered to many groups, one of which included:

- A secretary to the deceased professor

- A colleague who was working on a project with the professor
- A couple of students who knew the professor well and had him as an advisor
- Two seniors who had worked as the professor's graduate assistants for a couple of years
- One student who just really liked the professor because he had done something nice for her

Scenario 6

A man came into a residence hall around 9:00 p.m. and stabbed his ex-girlfriend to death. She lived on the second floor in a suite, and her suite-mates heard the fighting and the screaming. He also threatened them and they were terrified for their own safety. A resident assistant called security and an ambulance. Eight or nine floor-mates heard the screams and two of them saw the man running down the back stairs as the security officers were coming up the front stairs. The security officers apprehended the perpetrator 10 minutes after he left the building, following a foot race down college streets.

Interventions

Debriefings were provided the following evening. In attendance at the first session were: The suite-mates and the other students who lived in the dorm. A separate debriefing was provided for the security officers.

Scenario 7

This scenario involves the death of a sorority sister who attended a signing party and was forced to drink. In the early hours of the next morning she became unconscious in her room surrounded by her friends, roommates, and sorority sisters. They thought she had just passed out, but she never regained consciousness and died before they called 911.

Interventions

CISDs were provided for the house residents the next day and again after the funeral.

Scenario 8

The men's soccer team was returning to campus in personal automobiles after winning the division championships. A semitrailer truck hit some wet leaves and flipped over in front of one of the cars. This collision killed five junior students: the goalie, the captain, and three other members of the team. The car belonged to the goalie's girlfriend.

Interventions

Separate debriefings were provided the following day and after the funerals, for:

- The surviving members of the team, including the coach
- Members of the cheerleading team and the goalie's girlfriend
- Girlfriend/best friends of the deceased
- The remainder of the college campus

Scenario 9

A fatality occurred at an intramural sports event. A basketball player was talking to another student when he fell forward without any indication that there was anything wrong. His face struck the floor and blood flowed from his nose and mouth. Another student from the team ran over and started administering CPR. Police arriving on the scene used a defibrillator, then inserted a breathing tube. A member of the college's emergency medical services club worked on him as other members of the EMS service stood by. The city ambulance arrived and they shocked him again as he still was not breathing.

All these medical procedures were accomplished in front of his friends and teammates. The ambulance personnel then transported him to the hospital. Stunned students could not understand what had happened and the nature of the injury. Many of the student onlookers had never seen a dead person, much less someone their own age and one of their own friends.

Interventions

Debriefings were provided for the people at the scene:

- Team members
- Onlookers
- EMS and law enforcement personnel
- Dormitory residents from the hall in which the deceased resided

CMBs were provided for the college staff, faculty, students, and worried parents.

Scenarios of events where CIS Debriefings were provided:

(1) A cheerleader was thrown into the air and was not caught. The fall critically injured her back. (Debriefing for other cheerleaders.)

(2) While walking on a city street on her way back to the dorm, a woman was jumped from behind, dragged into the bushes, and raped. (Debriefing for other dorm residents.)

(3) A faculty member collapsed in a third-floor classroom and lost consciousness. Students could not find a phone on that floor to call 911, did not know CPR, and knew this woman was an adjunct faculty member and had no health insurance. The EMTs had a difficult time getting her down the winding staircase. (Debriefing provided to students in the class, the following day).

(4) An off-campus, older transfer student hanged himself. His girlfriend's mother had talked with him at 5:00 a.m., knew he was depressed and suicidal, and called 911. It took the ambulance a long time to arrive despite it being only three blocks from the fire station. The student worked at a nearby restaurant popular with the college crowd. He was also a fraternity brother. Many fraternity brothers and affiliated sorority sisters worked at this same restaurant. The apartment building where he died housed many college students. (Debriefings were provided for fellow workers, fellow residents, and family members.)

(5) A very popular resident assistant was killed in a single-car accident. He was a member of student government and well known and liked. Other RA's in the dorm were very shaken. Students on his floor were in disbelief. Resident directors across campus knew him and were themselves grieving at the same time they were trying to compose their staffs. The young man's girlfriend lived in a residence hall on campus. (Debriefings were provided for groups based on proximity to the event or the person.)

(6) Death of a female student off campus. She had been a healthy, vibrant, person who died in her sleep. An autopsy was being done the next day, as the cause of death was unknown. Four men lived in the house where her boyfriend lived (where she died); four women lived in her off-campus house down the street. (A debriefing was provided for those immediate friends.)

(7) During final exam time, someone set off the fire sprinklers in a dorm. By the time the fire department arrived about a dozen computers

were damaged and final papers were soaked. Students had take-home exams and final drafts of papers in their computers and on their desks. These computers were unsalvageable. Students were furious, scared, and frantic because of faculty expectations of end of the year assignments and exams. (Debriefings were provided to affected students, and to staff).

Points to Ponder:

1. If we forget a phase (like "What was your role?" or "What were you thinking at the time of the incident?") we can go back and address it (no one will know the difference!).
2. The teaching phase is as important as the introduction.
3. Stepping around the circle for each question/stage works well and is less time consuming than waiting for people voluntarily to articulate their thoughts and feelings.
4. The fact phase, or story-telling process, identifies everyone's role in the incident. During the pre-debriefing meeting, CISM team members need to know who was in charge of what. Rank does play a part in the scenario, although it does not in the debriefing. Be sure that the person in charge has extra support, if they need it.
5. People's vulnerabilities are accentuated at a time of intense crisis, and we are sometimes dealing with more than the reaction to the immediate situation at hand.
6. Those of us who are counselors/therapists need to stop our propensity to go deeper and encourage participants to say more or cry more. Remember Mitchell's rule: "If you ask more that two questions, it is psychotherapy. "
7. Make it very clear at the introduction that crisis intervention is not counseling or psychotherapy.
8. It is important to affirm their feelings, i.e., fear, anger, etc., and that these are natural reactions to an abnormal event.
9. Separate people into appropriate groups, based upon their distance from the event or the person involved; for example, those focusing more on the death of the professor in one group, those who were in the classroom building and themselves experienced the explosion, gas, etc., in another group.
10. In the re-entry phase, do not try to create a caring group, or community, of the people in the debriefing, if they do not know each other. Help move them along in their own journey of healing. Give space and time for individuals to voice plans before suggesting anything. It is most

powerful to evoke plans from the group and empower them to take action.

11. Be sure the group knows the team will be around to talk after the debriefing

12. Eye contact with individual members is critical. It is also important as a sign to the next member of the team to speak or be active.

13. Thanking individual members *by name* after they speak facilitates the process. Subtly, it helps to let them know that it is time for the next person to speak.

14. When setting up the team, be sure to ask each potential team member if there might be a personal reason to *not* want to be a member of this debriefing: example, personal experience of a suicide or recent personal crisis.

15. When doing intervention in an off-campus setting, pay attention to who invites you in to do the intervention. If there is a president or director, or person in charge other than the person who invites you in to do the intervention, be aware what that person knows about the intervention and what their relationship is with the rest of the staff.

16. When in the symptoms phrase, ask: "What are you experiencing? How do you know this event has affected you?"

17. An excellent thing to say is: "If you can just take away one thing from this conversation, that is important."

18. Reiterate the importance of confidentiality often, especially at the end.

References

Mitchell, J.T. & Everly, G. S., Jr. (2001). *Critical Incident Stress Debriefing: An Operations Manual for CISD, Defusing and Other Group Crisis Intervention Services, 3rd ed.,* (pp. 109-110). Ellicott City, MD: Chevron Publishing.

Index

A

activated team 9-10, 97-98, 100, 110, 122
Acute Stress Disorder (ASD) 15
administrative structure 94
alcohol 20, 62, 127
American Psychiatric Association 13, 15-16, 24, 42, 69, 86, 113, 120, 124, 139
American Psychological Association 25, 69, 125
anxiety 6, 14-15, 20, 22-24, 45, 50, 52, 76, 121
Assaulted Staff Action Program, The (ASAP) 113-125, 129
attending skills 65-67
attention 49-50

B

barriers to listening 65
burnout 30, 42

C

campus disaster plan 6
catecholamines 46-47, 50
chronic anxiety 20
CISD
see *Critical Incident Stress Debriefing*
CISM 7-10, 58, 68, 71-79, 81, 83-87, 90-99, 101-112, 114, 117, 120-121, 124-125, 128-129, 131, 138
also see *Critical Incident Stress Management*
CISM services 77, 91, 97, 105
clarification of alternatives 67
CMB 68, 74-77, 85
cognitive behavior therapy 22
combat fatigue 13
communications 89, 92, 98, 111
community response team 91
comorbidity 20, 24-25
compassion fatigue 30-31, 42-43
concentration 49-50, 55

congruent nonverbal expressions 67
corticosteriods 46, 50
counseling center 6-10, 62, 91, 94-95, 107-108, 121-122, 125-126, 128
counseling departments 90
countertransference 31-32, 43
Crisis Management Briefing (CMB) 9, 68, 72, 74, 76, 85, 103, 109, 110-111, 137
Crisis Response Team 72, 89, 91-92, 94-97, 100, 122, 129
Critical Incident Stress Debriefing (CISD) 8, 79, 82, 87, 98, 110, 117, 121, 131, 134-135
Critical Incident Stress Management (CISM) 7, 53, 57, 68, 71, 73, 85-87, 90-91, 103, 105, 114, 124-125
  also see CISM
crisis intervention
  see interventions
CRT
  see Crisis Response Team

D

deactivation of the team 96, 98
debriefing 7-9, 11, 21, 39, 72, 79-82, 85, 87, 93, 98, 100, 102, 110-112, 117, 126, 131, 133-139
defusing 9, 21, 72, 77-79, 85, 87, 98, 100, 110-111, 126, 139
depression 20, 24, 45, 54
detachment 15, 17-20, 35
Diagnostic and Statistical Manual (DSM-IV-TR) 13, 24, 30, 42, 86, 124
diagnostic criteria
  see Diagnostic and Statistical Manual
directory information 62
disasters 113, 115
  see man-made disasters
  natural disasters
dispatch office 108
dispatching 96-97, 109
dissociation 42, 47, 49
dissociative reactions 47, 49
divorce 20
drug abuse 20

E

education 26, 53, 55, 57, 59-63, 72-73, 92-94, 122

education records 59-62
EMDR
see eye movement desensitization and reprocessing
emotional numbing 19
endogenous opioids 46-47, 50
eye movement desensitization and reprocessing (EMDR) 23-26

F

Family Educational Rights and Privacy Act (FERPA)
see FERPA
Family Policy Compliance Office 61, 63
FERPA 59-63
flashbacks 15, 19, 22
follow-up 69-70, 72, 86, 98
funerals 110, 112, 136

G

goals of a crisis response team 9, 92
Gonzaga v. Doe 62
guilt 18, 20-22, 76, 132
Gustavus Adolphus College 1, 3-5, 7, 9, 11

H

hypervigilance 17-18, 20, 113, 117, 119

I

ICISF 8, 9, 72, 82, 91, 93
see International Critical Incident Stress Foundation
image 92
in vivo 23
Incident Command System 106
individual interventions 72, 82, 111
International Critical Incident Stress Foundation (ICISF) 9, 71-72
intervention techniques 72, 85, 96, 98, 100, 103, 112, 129
interventions 7, 9, 21, 53-54, 71-74, 77-79, 82, 84-86, 92, 98, 110-111, 114-116, 118, 120-121, 123, 125, 127, 129, 134-136

L

leadership 93
legal issues 94-95, 122
legitimate educational interest 60-61
Limbic system 48

M

medications 24
membership 92-94, 96, 99
memory 48-50, 55
Mental Health Infosource 69
Mental Health Net 69
mental health professionals 8, 10, 29, 39, 74, 76, 91, 95, 98, 100, 109-110
MentalHealth.com 69
MICCN 8-10, 97-98, 128
minimal encourages 65
Minnesota Inter-College Crisis Network (MICCN)
see MICCN

N

National Alliance for the Mentally Ill 69
National Association of Social Workers 69
natural disaster 2, 13-14, 16, 90
nonverbal communication 64

O

objective 7, 92
on-duty co-ordinator 109
operations manual 72, 96, 99

P

panic attacks 20
paraphrasing 65-66
parents 7, 59-65, 67-70, 75, 103, 107, 110, 118, 122, 128-129, 132, 137
peer support volunteers 55
perception checking 67
phobias 20
plan of action 64, 82, 92, 110
Posttraumatic Stress Disorder (PTSD)
see PTSD
preparedness 3
primary 3, 29, 31, 33, 92, 94
proper practices 96
PTSD 16, 19-32, 36, 42, 52, 54, 57, 120, 124, 126

R

rapid assessment syndrome 92
re-experiencing 15, 19
reassure 64, 92
referrals 69-70, 84, 86, 96, 100, 114, 117-118, 122
reflection of feeling 66
requests for elaboration 67
response 2-3, 5-10, 17, 39, 45-47, 50-51, 53, 56, 67, 71-75, 90-93, 96-98, 103, 113-114, 127-129
responsibility 7, 52, 61, 93-94, 96, 123

S

SAFE-R model 82, 84, 86
safety 6, 15, 37, 59, 60, 64, 71-72, 83, 89, 92, 94, 96, 98, 117, 120-121, 124, 126, 135
secondary 29, 31, 33, 50, 52, 92, 128
Secondary Traumatic Stress 30-32, 42-43
self-esteem 20
sexual assault 2, 13-16, 19, 22, 115
shell shock 13, 31
Social Intervention 55
social support 21, 31, 55, 115
startle reflex 49
student affairs 8, 10, 91, 94-95
student death 2, 9, 11
suicide 2, 10-11, 13, 20, 37, 56, 67, 76, 85, 90, 113, 121-122, 126-127, 134, 139
supporting skills 66-67
systematic desensitization 22-24

T

task force 91-92
tertiary 92
therapeutic interventions 21, 54
tornado 1-2, 4-10, 14, 18, 37, 59, 90, 128
training 8-10, 26, 34, 58, 86, 91-96, 99, 102, 114, 116, 122-123, 128, 131
traumatic event 14-17, 19, 21, 23-24, 30-39, 48-49, 53, 55, 59, 72, 89, 90, 117, 128
traumatic stress disorder 13-18, 21-27, 29-31, 45, 48, 57-58, 73, 108, 112-113, 124, 128

U

U.S. Department of Education 60-61, 63
unemployment 20

V

vicarious trauma 29-39

W

warning signs of trauma related stress 14-15
working with groups of parents 68